MOTHER GOOSE READERS THEATRE FOR BEGINNING READERS

RECENT TITLES IN TEACHER IDEAS PRESS' READERS THEATRE SERIES

MOTHER GOOSE READERS THEATRE FOR BEGINNING READERS

Anthony D. Fredericks

Readers Theatre

Teacher Ideas Press

An imprint of Libraries Unlimited
Westport, Connecticut • London

Library of Congress Cataloging-in-Publication Data

Fredericks, Anthony D.
  Mother Goose readers theatre for beginning readers / Anthony D. Fredericks.
    p. cm. — (Readers theatre)
  Includes bibliographical references and index.
  ISBN-13: 978-1-59158-500-8 (alk. paper)
  ISBN-10: 1-59158-500-7 (alk. paper)
  1. Readers' theater. 2. Drama in education. 3. Children's plays. 4. Mother Goose. 5. Activity programs in education. I. Title.
  PN2081.R4F742 2007
  372.66—dc22 2006103023

British Library Cataloguing in Publication Data is available.

Library of Congress Catalog Card Number: 2006103023
ISBN: 978-1-59158-500-8

First published in 2007

Libraries Unlimited/Teacher Ideas Press, 88 Post Road West, Westport, CT 06881
A Member of the Greenwood Publishing Group, Inc.
www.lu.com

Printed in the United States of America

∞™

The paper used in this book complies with the
Permanent Paper Standard issued by the National
Information Standards Organization (Z39.48–1984).

10 9 8 7 6 5 4 3 2 1

To Judy Wolfman—for all the laughter, literature, and wonderful Once Upon a Time times!

Contents

Part II
Reading Level, Second Grade

Preface

This Rhymin' Teacher
(sung to "This Little Piggy")

This rhymin' teacher read poetry.
This rhymin' teacher sang a song.
This rhymin' teacher made music.
This rhymin' teacher danced along.
And all their students cried,
"Hurray! Hurray! Hurray!"
All the day long!

Mother Goose rhymes have been a staple of children's literature ever since they were first published in seventeenth-century France. For many children they are their earliest introduction to the playfulness of language—the flow, meter, and cadence of words and phrases. Mother Goose rhymes invite children to actively participate by singing, clapping, or jumping up and down to the rhythm of a jingle:

One, two, buckle my shoe.
Three, four, knock at the door.
Five, six, pick up sticks.
Seven, eight, lay them straight.
Nine, ten, a good fat hen.

Rhyming is a familiar aspect of most Mother Goose verses. Often the rhyme patterns are silly—a feature that indicates to children the fun that can be had with words. Other times the rhyming patterns encourage listeners to create their own words or endings to lines—a further inducement to be active participants in the telling of a story.

Alliteration is another familiar feature of Mother Goose rhymes. The repetition of initial consonant sounds is one of the earliest phonemic awareness skills children master, and with Mother Goose rhymes they can hear those repetitive sounds in action:

Peter Piper picked a peck of pickled peppers;
A peck of pickled peppers Peter Piper picked.
If Peter Piper picked a peck of pickled peppers,
Where's the peck of pickled peppers Peter Piper picked?

Certainly, one of the most endearing qualities of Mother Goose rhymes is their overt humor. Characters fall down hills, bring farm animals to school, stick their thumbs into pastry products, and leap over celestial objects. The situations are ridiculous, exaggerated, and simply silly—just the kind of humor young kids love!

This book offers beginning readers a participatory approach to the wide and wonderful world of Mother Goose rhymes. It is based on the idea that when students are provided with meaningful opportunities to make an "investment in self" in their education, that education will become both relevant and dynamic. *Mother Goose Readers Theatre for Beginning Readers* presents readers theatre scripts that stimulate children to become active participants in popular and familiar rhymes. Students will examine tales, explore stories, and investigate cherished rhymes that are staples of their early literary experiences. In short, students will enact Mother Goose rhymes that are engaging, delightful, and full of fun!

Within these pages is a dynamic variety of creative learning possibilities for your classroom. Here, your students will discover an exciting cornucopia of mind-expanding and concept-building experiences—experiences that will engage and excite them as beginning readers. Just as important —your students will participate in positive learning experiences that can serve as a strong foundation for additional literary explorations in phonemic awareness, phonics, fluency, vocabulary, and comprehension development.

So, be prepared for lots of action, lots of drama, and lots of fun!

A teacher—Miss Muffet
Sat on her tuffet,
Watching a Mother Goose play.
The children were joyous:
All the girls and the boy-us,
And they all had a great learning day!

—Tony Fredericks

Acknowledgments

Throughout this extraordinary literary venture, I have been supported and encouraged by many individuals. They each deserve a thunderous round of applause, a plethora of "high fives," and a shower of raucous cheers!

I am especially indebted to Mallori Gillespie, who worked under an extremely tight deadline to provide the Spanish translations for several designated scripts. Her enthusiasm for this project is sincerely appreciated and valued. She made sure each and every script maintained its humor, theme, and intent. Thank you, Mallori!

I am equally indebted to Dolka Lugo, who meticulously checked and verified the accuracy of the Spanish translations. Her contributions are equally valued!

To my longtime friends and colleagues—Paula Gilbert and Judy Wolfman—who were co-partners with me in an extraordinary program of children's books, storytelling, and magical interactions with underserved urban youngsters, I am particularly grateful. Their continuing support and enormous energy are always treasured . . . always celebrated. They truly bring life to literature and literature to life.

And, to all the teachers throughout Canada, Mexico, and the United States who have used my previous readers theatre books in your classrooms—thank you! The energy you have shared and the stories your students have told are treasured memories of this fantastic literary venture—a journey of wondrous possibilities and a voyage of incredible imagination.

Introduction

Once upon a time, in 1997, I wrote a teacher resource book called *Tadpole Tales and Other Totally Terrific Treats for Readers Theatre* (Teacher Ideas Press)—a book that was specifically designed for teachers in grades 1–3 (all of the scripts were controlled for readability). That book was a collection of "wild and wacky" readers theatre scripts that were adaptations of familiar rhymes and traditional fairy tales. Titles of some of the scripts in that book included:

- ❖ "One, Two, Buckle My Shoe. Three, Four, Mommy Can Snore"

- ❖ "Goldilocks and the Three Hamsters"

- ❖ "The Big Bad Pig and the Three Little Wolves"

- ❖ "Little Bo-Peep Has Lost Her Sheep and All Her Lunch Money, Too"

- ❖ "Old King Cole Was a Merry Old Soul Until He Had to Do His Math Homework"

That book found its way into thousands of primary-level classrooms and library programs around the country. Teachers would use it as a major part of their language arts program. Librarians would buy it and use it to introduce classic stories as part of their regular library offerings. It soon became a popular and much-loved part of children's initial introductions to literature and learning.

Letters, e-mails, and comments I received from educators across the country attested to the unbelievable joy that came about when readers theatre was made part of classroom and library experiences. Typically, those messages celebrated three specific benefits of readers theatre:

1. **Fluency**—"I really like the way readers theatre provides my first grade students with positive models of language use that help build bridges between word recognition and comprehension."

2. **Integrated language arts**—"When children (during library time) participate in readers theatre they can understand and appreciate the interrelationships between reading, writing, listening, and speaking . . . and literature!"

3. **English Language Learners**—"My ELL students benefit from readers theatre because they can see and hear language in action as well as the various ways in which English is used—by me and the other students."

With the success of *Tadpole Tales . . . ,* it wasn't too long before teachers and librarians would approach me at conferences and teacher in-service presentations asking for a new volume of readers theatre scripts. They not only requested scripts that could be used with beginning readers, but were equally interested in scripts that celebrated classic literature—specifically Mother Goose rhymes. Thus was born the idea for this book.

WHAT IS READERS THEATRE?

Readers theatre is a storytelling device that stimulates the imagination and promotes *all* of the language arts. Simply stated, it is an oral interpretation of a piece of literature read in a dramatic style. Readers theatre is an act of involvement, an opportunity to share, a time to creatively interact with others, and a personal interpretation of what can be or could be. Readers theatre provides numerous opportunities for youngsters to make stories and literature come alive and pulsate with their own unique brand of perception and vision. In so doing, literature becomes personal and reflective—children have a breadth of opportunities to be authentic users of language.

The magic of storytelling has been a tradition of every culture and civilization since the dawn of language. It binds human beings and celebrates their heritage as no other language art can. It is part and parcel of the human experience, because it underscores the values and experiences we cherish as well as those we seek to share with each other. Nowhere is this more important than in today's classroom. Perhaps it is a natural part of who we are—that stories command our attention and help us appreciate the values, ideas, and traditions we hold dear. So, too, should students have those same experiences and those same pleasures.

Storytelling conjures up all sorts of visions and possibilities—faraway lands, magnificent adventures, enchanted princes, beautiful princesses, evil wizards and wicked witches, a few dragons and demons, a couple of castles and cottages, perhaps a mysterious forest or two, and certainly tales of mystery, intrigue, and adventure. These are stories of tradition and timelessness, tales that enchant, mystify, and excite through a marvelous weaving of characters, settings, and plots . . . tales that have stood the test of time. Our senses are stimulated, our mental images are energized, and our experiences are fortified through the magic of storytelling.

Storytelling is also a way of sharing the power and intrigue of language. I suppose part of my belief that storytelling is the quintessential classroom activity lies in the fact that it is an opportunity to bring life, vitality, and substance to the two-dimensional letters and words on a printed page. So, too, is it an interpersonal activity—a "never-fail" way to connect with minds and souls and hearts.

When children are provided with regular opportunities to become storytellers, they develop a personal stake in the literature shared. They also begin to cultivate personal interpretations of that literature—interpretations that lead to higher levels of appreciation and comprehension. Practicing and performing stories is an involvement endeavor—one that demonstrates and utilizes numerous languaging activities. So, too, do youngsters learn to listen to their classmates and appreciate a variety of presentations.

READERS THEATRE AND FLUENCY

Of no less importance is the significance of readers theatre as a method to enhance reading fluency. Reading researchers have identified five primary areas of reading instruction for all beginning readers: phonemic awareness, phonics, fluency, vocabulary, and comprehension. When teachers and librarians incorporate readers theatre into their respective programs, youngsters are offered multiple opportunities to, as one first-grade teacher put it, "understand the rhythm and flow of language."

Fluency is the ability to read text accurately and quickly. It's reading in which words are recognized automatically. When fluent readers read, they group words quickly to help them gain meaning from what they read. Their oral reading sounds natural and their silent reading is smooth and unencumbered by an overemphasis on word-by-word analysis. Fluent readers are those who do not need to concentrate on the decoding of words; rather, they can direct their attention to their comprehension of text. In short, fluent readers are able to recognize words and comprehend them at the same time. They are able to make connections between their background knowledge and ideas in a book or other piece of writing. I often like to think of fluency as the essential stepping stone between phonetic ability and comprehension.

It's important to remember that fluency is something that develops over time. Fluency instruction must be integrated into all aspects of the reading program as the "bridge" that students need to be successful comprehenders. Fluency is not an isolated element of the reading curriculum—rather, it is an essential component that models and provides active involvement opportunities for students as they transition from decoding to comprehension. A recent study by the National Assessment of Educational Progress (2001) found a direct correlation between fluency and reading comprehension. In fact, students who score low on measures of fluency also score low on measures of comprehension. The implication was that efforts designed to foster fluency development will have a direct impact on students' growth and development in comprehension.

Not surprising, one of the most effective ways teachers can promote fluency development—particularly for beginning readers—is through the use of readers theatre. Its advantages are twofold:

1.   it offers positive models of fluent reading as demonstrated by a teacher or other accomplished readers, and

2.   it provides beginning readers with a legitimate reason for rereading text in an enjoyable and engaging format.

Students get to practice fluency in authentic texts and in authentic situations. Reading is portrayed as a pleasurable activity—it has both purpose and interest. As students take on the roles of characters, they also take on the roles of competent readers.

WHAT IS THE VALUE OF READERS THEATRE?

I like to think of readers theatre as a way to interpret literature without the constraints of skills, rote memorization, or assignments. Readers theatre allows children to breathe life and substance into stories—an interpretation that is colored by kids' unique perspectives, experiences, and vision. It is, in fact, the readers' interpretation of an event that is intrinsically more valuable than some predetermined and/or preordained "translation" (something that might be found in a teacher's manual or curriculum guide, for example).

With that in mind, I'd like to share with you some of the many values I see in readers theatre:

❖ Readers theatre is a participatory event. The characters as well as the audience are all intimately involved in the design, structure, and delivery of the story. As such, children begin to realize that learning is not a solitary activity, but one that can be shared and discussed with others.

❖ Readers theatre stimulates curiosity and enthusiasm for learning. It allows children to experience learning in a supportive and nonthreatening format that underscores their active involvement.

❖ Since it is the performance that drives readers theatre, children are given more opportunities to invest themselves and their personalities in the production of a readers theatre. The same story may be subject to several different presentations depending on the group or the individual youngsters involved. As such, children learn that readers theatre can be explored in a host of ways and a host of possibilities.

❖ Readers theatre is informal and relaxed. It does not require elaborate props, scenery, or costumes. It can be set up in any classroom or library. It does not require large sums of money to "make it happen." And, it can be "put on" in any kind of environment—formal or informal.

❖ Readers theatre stimulates the imagination and the creation of visual images. It has been substantiated that when youngsters are provided with opportunities to create their own mental images, their comprehension and appreciation of a piece of writing will be enhanced considerably. Since only a modicum of formal props and "set up" are required for any readers theatre production, the participants and audience are encouraged to create supplemental "props" in their minds—props that may be more elaborate and exquisite than those found in the most lavish of plays.

❖ Readers theatre enhances the development of cooperative learning strategies. It requires youngsters to work together toward a common goal and supports their efforts in doing so. Readers theatre is not a competitive activity, but rather a cooperative one in which children share, discuss, and band together for the good of the production.

❖ Teachers and librarians have also discovered that readers theatre is an excellent way in which to enhance the development of communication skills. Voice projection, intonation, inflection, and pronunciation skills are all promoted within and throughout any readers theatre production.

❖ The development and enhancement of self-concept is facilitated through readers theatre. Since children are working in concert with other children in a supportive atmosphere, their self-esteem mushrooms accordingly. Again, the emphasis is on the presentation, not necessarily the performers. As such, youngsters have opportunities to develop levels of self-confidence and self-assurance that would not normally be available in more traditional class productions.

❖ Creative and critical thinking are enhanced through the utilization of readers theatre. Children are active participants in the interpretation and delivery of a story; as such, they develop thinking skills that are divergent rather than convergent, and interpretive skills that are supported rather than directed.

❖ Readers theatre is fun! Children of all ages have delighted in using readers theatre for many years. It is delightful and stimulating, encouraging and fascinating, relevant and personal. Indeed, try as I might, I have not been able to locate a single instance (or group of children) in which (or for whom) readers theatre would not be an appropriate learning activity. It is a strategy filled with a cornucopia of possibilities and promises.

Readers theatre holds the promise of "energizing" your classroom language arts curriculum, stimulating your library program, and fostering an active and deeper engagement of students in all the dynamics of books, literature, and reading. For both classroom teachers and school librarians, its benefits are enormous and its implications endless.

Please check out the companion book: *Nonfiction Readers Theatre for Beginning Readers* (Teacher Ideas Press, 2007).

Presentation Suggestions

It is important to remember that there is no single way to present readers theatre. What follows are some ideas you and the youngsters with whom you work may wish to keep in mind as you put on the productions in this book—whether in a classroom setting or the school library.

PREPARING SCRIPTS

One of the advantages of using readers theatre in the classroom is the lack of extra work or preparation time necessary to get "up and running." By using the scripts in this book, your preparation time is minimal.

❖ After a script has been selected for presentation, make sufficient copies. A copy of the script should be provided for each actor. In addition, making two or three extra copies (one for you and "replacement" copies for scripts that are accidentally damaged or lost) is also a good idea. Copies for the audience are unnecessary and are not suggested.

❖ Each script can be bound between two sheets of colored construction paper or poster board. Bound scripts tend to formalize the presentation a little and lend an air of professionalism to the actors.

❖ Highlight each character's speaking parts with different color highlighter pens. This helps youngsters track their parts without being distracted by the dialogue of others.

❖ After duplicating the necessary number of English/Spanish scripts (according to the designated number of characters), use a highlighter pen to highlight all of the English lines or all of the Spanish lines (as applicable) in each copy of the script. Then instruct the students to focus solely on the blue lines (or green lines, or pink lines, etc.) in their reading of the script. This will help keep them focused on just the English lines or Spanish lines (as appropriate).

STARTING OUT

Introducing the concept of readers theatre to your students for the first time may be as simple as sharing a script with the entire class and "walking" youngsters through the design and delivery of that script.

❖ Emphasize that a readers theatre performance does not require any memorization of the script. It's the interpretation and performance that count.

❖ You may wish to read through an entire script aloud, taking on the various roles. Let students know how easy and comfortable this process is.

❖ Encourage selected volunteers to read assigned parts of a sample script to the entire class. Readers should stand or sit in a circle so that other classmates can observe them.

❖ Provide opportunities for additional rereadings using other volunteers. Plan time to discuss the ease of presentation and the different interpretations offered by different readers.

From *Mother Goose Readers Theatre for Beginning Readers* by Anthony D. Fredericks. Westport, CT: Teacher Ideas Press. Copyright © 2007 by Anthony D. Fredericks.

- ❖ Readers should have an opportunity to practice their script before presenting it to an audience. Take some time to discuss voice intonation, facial gestures, body movements, and other features that could be used to enhance the presentation.

- ❖ Allow children the opportunity to suggest their own modifications, adaptations, or interpretations of the script. They will undoubtedly be "in tune" with the interests and perceptions of their peers and can offer some distinctive and personal interpretations.

- ❖ Encourage students to select nonstereotypical roles within any readers theatre script. For example, boys can take on female roles and girls can take on male roles, the smallest person in the class can take on the role of a giant dinosaur, a shy student can take on the role of a boastful, bragging giant. Provide sufficient opportunities for students to expand and extend their appreciation of readers theatre through a variety of "out of character" roles.

STAGING

Staging involves the physical location of the readers as well as any necessary movements. Unlike a more formal play, the movements are often minimal. The emphasis is more on presentation and less on action.

- ❖ For most presentations, readers will stand and/or sit on stools or chairs. The physical location of each reader has been indicated for each of the scripts in this book.

- ❖ If there are many characters in the presentation, it may be advantageous to have characters in the rear (upstage) standing while those in the front (downstage) are placed on stools or chairs. This ensures that the audience will both see and hear each actor.

- ❖ Usually all of the characters will be on stage throughout the duration of the presentation. For most presentations it is not necessary to have characters enter and exit the presentation. If you place the characters on stools, they can face the audience when they are involved in a particular scene and then turn around whenever they are not involved in a scene.

- ❖ You may wish to make simple hand-lettered signs with the name of each character. Loop a piece of string or yarn through each sign and hang it around the neck of each respective character. That way, the audience will know the identity of each character throughout the presentation.

- ❖ Each reader will have her or his own copy of the script in a paper cover (see above). If possible, use a music stand for each reader's script (this allows readers to use their hands for dramatic interpretations as necessary).

- ❖ Several presentations have a narrator to set up the story. The narrator serves to establish the place and time of the story for the audience so that the characters can "jump into" their parts from the beginning of the story. Typically, the narrator is separated from the other "actors" and can be identified by a simple sign.

PROPS

Two of the positive features of readers theatre are its ease of preparation and its ease of presentation. Informality is a hallmark of any readers theatre script.

❖ Much of the setting for a story should take place in the audience's mind. Elaborate scenery is not necessary—simple props are often the best. For example:

  – A branch or potted plant can serve as a tree.

  – A drawing on the chalkboard can illustrate a building.

  – A hand-lettered sign can designate one part of the staging area as a particular scene (e.g., swamp, castle, field, forest).

  – Children's toys can be used for uncomplicated props (e.g., telephone, vehicles, etc.).

  – A sheet of aluminum foil or a remnant of blue cloth can be used to simulate a lake or pond.

❖ Costumes for the actors are unnecessary. A few simple items may be suggested by students. For example:

  – Hats, scarves, or aprons can be used by major characters.

  – A paper cutout can serve as a tie, button, or badge.

  – Old clothing (borrowed from parents) can be used as warranted.

❖ Some teachers and librarians have discovered that the addition of appropriate background music or sound effects can enhance a readers theatre presentation.

❖ It's important to remember that the emphasis in readers theatre is on the reading—not on any accompanying "features." The best presentations are often the simplest.

DELIVERY

I've often found it advantageous to let students know that the only difference between a readers theatre presentation and a movie role is the fact that they will have a script in their hands. This allows them to focus more on presenting rather than memorizing a script.

❖ When first introduced to readers theatre, students often have a tendency to "read into" their scripts. Encourage students to look up from their scripts and interact with other characters or the audience as necessary

❖ Practicing the script beforehand can eliminate the problem of students burying their heads in the pages. In so doing, children understand the need to involve the audience as much as possible in the development of the story.

❖ Voice projection and delivery are important in allowing the audience to understand character actions. The proper mood and intent needs to be established—aspects that are possible when children are familiar and comfortable with each character's "style."

❖ Again, the emphasis is on delivery, so be sure to suggest different types of voice (e.g., angry, irritated, calm, frustrated, excited, etc.) that children may wish to use for their particular character(s).

From *Mother Goose Readers Theatre for Beginning Readers* by Anthony D. Fredericks. Westport, CT: Teacher Ideas Press. Copyright © 2007 by Anthony D. Fredericks.

ENGLISH LANGUAGE LEARNERS (ELL)

Children who are learning English as a second language face numerous challenges—challenges that native speakers seldom encounter. For example, students whose native language is Spanish pronounce selected letters (especially vowels) quite differently than English-speaking children. In Spanish, all the consonants (with the exception of *h*) are sounded, whereas in English there are several silent consonants (e.g., *k* as in knot, *g* as in gnu, *w* as in write).

Readers theatre offers ELL students a practical model of language use—one that can help them make the transition from their native language to English. Here are a few points to consider:

❖ For eight scripts in this book, there are Spanish versions. Invite your ELL students to present the Spanish version of a script immediately after an "English presentation."

❖ Invite ELL students to "teach" a Spanish version of a script to non-Spanish-speaking students.

❖ Use the Spanish scripts as read-aloud opportunities for all students. After reading a Spanish script, read its English equivalent to students.

❖ Tape record selected scripts (in English) and invite ELL students to follow along with a printed version.

❖ Use words from the English scripts along with their equivalents from the Spanish scripts to construct bilingual flash cards and word walls for children.

POST-PRESENTATION

As a wise author once said, "The play's the thing." So it is with readers theatre. In other words, the mere act of presenting a readers theatre script is complete in and of itself. It is not necessary, or even required, to do any type of formalized evaluation after readers theatre. Once again, the emphasis is on informality. Readers theatre should and can be a pleasurable and stimulating experience for children.

What follows are a few ideas you may want to share with students. In doing so, you will be providing youngsters with important learning opportunities that extend and promote all aspects of your language arts program.

❖ After a presentation, discuss with students how the script enhanced or altered the original story.

❖ Invite students to suggest other characters who could be added to the script.

❖ Invite students to suggest new or alternate dialogue for various characters

❖ Invite students to suggest new or different setting(s) for the script.

❖ Invite students to talk about their reactions to various characters' expressions, tone of voice, presentations, or dialogues.

❖ After a presentation, invite youngsters to suggest any modifications or changes needed in the script.

Presenting a readers theatre script need not be an elaborate or extensive production. As children become more familiar and polished in using readers theatre, they will be able to suggest a multitude of presentation possibilities for future scripts. It is important to help children assume a measure of self-initiated responsibility in the delivery of any readers theatre. In so doing, you will be helping to ensure their personal engagement and active participation in this most valuable of language arts activities.

Bonus Features

This resource has been especially designed for classroom teachers, school librarians, or reading specialists who work with beginning readers; specifically youngsters in grades 1–2. Teaching children in these grades has always been a challenge, yet the opportunities for literacy growth and development are enormous. Readers theatre has proven itself as one way you can help children learn language in context in addition to enhancing your overall reading or language arts program.

To help make your task of teaching primary-level youngsters a little easier, several bonus features have been included throughout the book. Please consider these as important elements in the introduction and use of readers theatre in your classroom or library.

READABILITY

Each of the scripts in this book has been assessed according to its readability—or its appropriateness for a specific reading grade level. You will discover 12 scripts written at the first-grade reading level and 12 scripts at the second-grade level. The primary factors in determining the readability of a script were sentence length and average number of syllables per word. With this in mind, you will be able to use scripts that are appropriate for the reading level of an entire class or for selected individuals within a class. However, you should also feel free to use scripts from both levels with your students.

SCRIPTS IN SPANISH

In each of the two parts of this book there are four Spanish scripts, each an exact translation of the English script in which it is integrated (total, eight scripts). You are encouraged to use these scripts with both your ELL students and your English-speaking students. In addition to the suggestions offered above (in the "English Language Learners (ELL)" section), here are some additional ideas you may wish to consider regarding these specific scripts.

❖ Use selected words from the Spanish scripts as "sight words" for your English-speaking students. Post these on an appropriate bulletin board.

❖ Provide students with "mini-lessons" in Spanish to help them learn the language of the ELL students in the class.

❖ Invite English-speaking students to present an "English" script to be followed by the "Spanish" equivalent immediately thereafter.

❖ Reverse the sequence of presentation as described above.

❖ Invite both English-speaking and ELL students to present an English script. Follow up by asking selected parent volunteers to present the Spanish equivalent to the class.

❖ Reverse the sequence above by asking parent volunteers to present an English script with a student follow-up of the Spanish script.

❖ Invite parent volunteers to make audiorecordings of both the English and Spanish scripts. Provide opportunities for students to listen to these recordings in their free time.

❖ Pair up English-speaking students with ELL "buddies" for informal tutoring sessions using the scripts in this book.

Please note that in translating the scripts from English to Spanish, the rhyming patterns of the Mother Goose stories was lost. Please indicate to your students that the "message" and fun of each story has been maintained in the Spanish scripts; however, the words used at the end of each line of a Mother Goose tale do not rhyme (in Spanish).

PHONEMIC AWARENESS

The relationship between phonemic awareness and reading instruction is considerable. Without proficiency in phonemic awareness, children may not have the necessary foundation for later reading competency. Numerous classroom studies have conclusively supported the fact that phonemic awareness is a necessary prerequisite for learning to read. Exposure to the oral sounds of language helps children prepare for dealing with the written forms of language. Interestingly, children who receive phonemic awareness training in kindergarten and first grade do significantly better on all measures of formal reading achievement (throughout their educational careers) when compared with children who do not receive such training.

For each script in Part I (First Grade), there is one or more phonemic awareness activities for you to share with children. They are offered to help you extend learning opportunities for your students by establishing a sense of "comfortableness" with the oral sounds of language. These activities are designed to enhance children's experiences with spoken language—hearing and recognizing certain sounds, identifying and understanding the way sounds are sequenced in words, and noting and learning about the role of phonemes in word construction.

Please keep in mind that phonemic awareness instruction should be but one element in an overall literacy program. The activities in this section of each readers theatre script are designed to offer you an array of learning possibilities for engaging students in the playfulness of language. Here are a few ideas for your consideration:

• Keep the emphasis on informality and playfulness. Let children know that phonemic awareness activities, just like the presentation of readers theatre scripts, are a fun way to play with language.

• Limit any instruction in phonemic awareness to 15 minutes per day. There is sufficient research indicating that any more time is nonproductive.

• Plan to share a wide variety of phonemic awareness activities with students—as part of their experiences with readers theatre as well as a separate learning venture.

• You may choose to introduce a particular activity to your students prior to sharing a readers theatre script. Or, you may elect to use a specific activity at the conclusion of a particular script. For best results, however, use a combination of pre- and post-script phonemic awareness activities.

• Listen carefully to the language used by children in everyday situations. Take advantage of that language and incorporate it into your own phonemic awareness activities.

• Keep in mind that the activities and suggestions throughout this book can be viewed as generic in nature. In short, please feel free to use your own words, the words of children in your classroom, or words from a district- or state-mandated list. Even better, plan regular opportunities to utilize words from the stories and literature you share with children each day.

- Just like readers theatre, phonemic awareness activities work best when they are promoted as group-based activities. Lots of interaction among students is the key to their success.

- Don't just limit phonemic awareness to a specific time of the day, but rather take advantage of the unplanned and informal opportunities that arise naturally (those "teachable moments"). Times when children line up for lunch, story time, indoor recess, and "Show and Tell" are but a few of the many opportunities you'll have to include some playful language activities.

- It's important for children to hear the sounds of language in natural contexts. Use children's literature (as well as the scripts in this book) as a way to introduce and emphasize phonemic awareness in an authentic way. Read to children regularly, stopping every so often to note the sounds in a word, the alliteration of letters, funny or unusual rhymes, or a distinctive arrangement of syllables. The trade books you normally share with children can be positive components of your phonemic awareness program.

All of the activities in Part I have been classroom-tested and "kid approved." All are designed to offer you and your students some wonderful adventures and exciting discoveries about the sounds of language.

COMPREHENSION STRATEGIES

Most educators hold to the belief that reading involves an active and energetic relationship between the reader and the text. This is a reciprocal relationship—one that includes characteristics of the reader as well as the nature of the materials. Reading researchers often refer to this as the *transactional approach to reading*—one in which readers interact positively with the text.

This view of reading is based on several critical features, including the following:

- All readers have experiences and prior knowledge that determines how well they will understand a text.

- Reading is not a passive activity—it involves aspects of the text just as much as it involves aspects of the reader.

- Because readers all have different experiences and different interpretations, there is no single way of interpreting a text.

Transactional reading places an emphasis on three critical and interrelated stages in the reading process. These stages work in a coordinated fashion to promote and enhance comprehension development for all readers:

1. **Before reading**—Processes designed to link students' background knowledge and experiences to the text.

2. **During reading**—Processes designed to help students read constructively and to interact with the text.

3. **After reading**—Processes designed to deepen and extend students' responses to text.

The scripts in Part II of this book provide you with selected comprehension activities that encourage and stimulate students to take an active role in their own comprehension development. Several strategies are provided that engage youngsters in thinking about the scripts, linking the stories with their backgrounds or experience, and predicting and inferring actions and results. Specifically, students are provided with opportunities to

- activate prior knowledge before, during, and after reading;

- connect the known with the unknown;

- use concrete or past experiences to create "mind pictures" or visual images;

- make "educated guesses" to form conclusions, make critical judgments, and create unique interpretations;

- predict future events in text;

- ask questions of themselves, the authors, and the texts they read;

- observe teachers as they model appropriate question-asking strategies;

- determine the most important ideas and themes in a text;

- group or classify ideas into recognizable categories;

- synthesize and summarize what they read; and

- rethink what they encounter in text.

The comprehension activities/strategies included in this book have been developed in cooperation with teachers in grades 1 and 2. Although they are provided for the scripts in Part II, you are certainly encouraged to use them in conjunction with scripts in Part I, too. In doing so, you will be providing students with unique and valuable opportunities to interact with text—specifically Mother Goose stories.

References

Fredericks, Anthony D. 1993. *Frantic Frogs and Other Frankly Fractured Folktales for Readers Theatre*. Westport, CT: Teacher Ideas Press.

———. 1997. *Tadpole Tales and Other Totally Terrific Treats for Readers Theatre*. Westport, CT: Teacher Ideas Press.

———. 2000. *Silly Salamanders and Other Slightly Stupid Stories for Readers Theatre*. Westport, CT: Teacher Ideas Press.

———. 2001. *Readers Theatre for American History*. Westport, CT: Teacher Ideas Press.

———. 2002. *Science Fiction Readers Theatre*. Westport, CT: Teacher Ideas Press.

———. 2007. *Nonfiction Readers Theatre for Beginning Readers*. Westport, CT: Teacher Ideas Press.

PART I

READING LEVEL, FIRST GRADE

Old Macdonald

PRESENTATION SUGGESTIONS

The six characters can be seated on chairs or standing in a loose semicircle. The presentation is the actual script for the original rhyme—no additional words or phrases have been added.

PROPS

This script does not require any props. However, you may wish to post some illustrations of farm scenes or farm animals behind the players for some added effect.

DELIVERY

The delivery should be upbeat and at a quick tempo (some practice may be necessary).

ORIGINAL VERSION

Old MacDonald had a farm, E-I-E-I-O
And on this farm he had some cows, E-I-E-I-O
With a moo-moo here, and a moo-moo there,
Here a moo, there a moo, everywhere a moo-moo.
Old MacDonald had a farm, E-I-E-I-O
And on this farm he had some donkeys, E-I-E-I-O

With a hee-haw here, and a hee-haw there,
Here a hee, there a haw, everywhere a hee-haw.

Old MacDonald had a farm, E-I-E-I-O.
And on this farm he had some pigs, E-I-E-I-O.
With an oink-oink here and an oink-oink there,
Here an oink, there an oink, everywhere an oink-oink.

Old MacDonald had a farm, E-I-E-I-O.
And on this farm he had some ducks, E-I-E-I-O.
With a quack-quack here and a quack-quack there,
Here a quack, there a quack, everywhere a quack-quack.

Old MacDonald had a farm, E-I-E-I-O.

PHONEMIC AWARENESS ACTIVITY(IES)

1. Repeat the first four lines of the rhyme and invite students to clap once after you say each word (or sound). Repeat several times. Change the first four lines to the following two rhymes, and invite children to repeat the activity by clapping once after each word.

    Old Miss Pork Chop had a house, E-I-E-I-O
    And in this house she had a rabbit, E-I-E-I-O
    With a chomp-chomp here and a chomp-chomp there.
    Here a chomp, there a chomp, everywhere a chomp-chomp.

    Old man Parker had a zoo, E-I-E-I-O
    And in this zoo he had a lion, E-I-E-I-O
    With a roar-roar here and a roar-roar there.
    Here a roar, there a roar, everywhere a roar-roar.

    Invite children to note that each word or word part resulted in a single clap (each word or word part was a single syllable).

2. After reading the rhyme several times, use a classroom puppet to say each of the following words in parts. Invite children to listen carefully and say the word as a whole:

    /m/ /a/ /n/ (man)
    /m/ /i/ /s/ /s/ (miss)
    /h/ /a/ /d/ (had)
    /l/ /i/ /o/ /n/ (lion)

Old MacDonald

El Viejo MacDonald

STAGING: There is no narrator for this story, nor do any of the characters have a name (they are simply designated by numbers). The characters may stand around in a loose circle or be seated on chairs in a semicircle facing the audience.

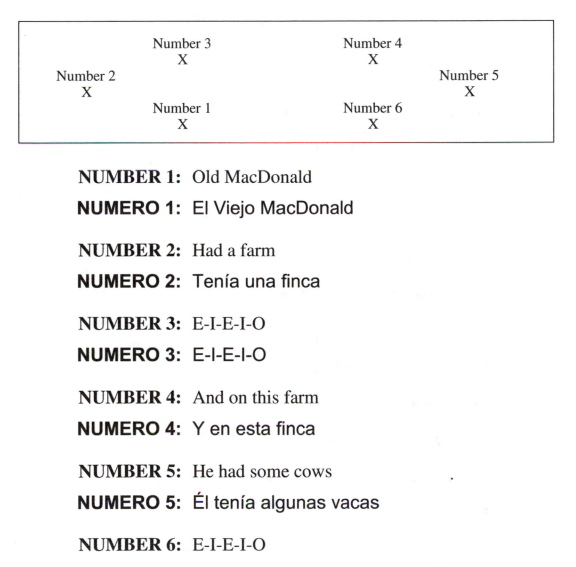

NUMBER 1: Old MacDonald

NUMERO 1: El Viejo MacDonald

NUMBER 2: Had a farm

NUMERO 2: Tenía una finca

NUMBER 3: E-I-E-I-O

NUMERO 3: E-I-E-I-O

NUMBER 4: And on this farm

NUMERO 4: Y en esta finca

NUMBER 5: He had some cows

NUMERO 5: Él tenía algunas vacas

NUMBER 6: E-I-E-I-O

NUMERO 6: E-I-E-I-O

NUMBER 1: With a moo-moo here
NUMERO 1: Con un mú-mú aquí

NUMBER 2: And a moo-moo there
NUMERO 2: Y un mú-mú allá

NUMBER 3: Here a moo
NUMERO 3: Aquí un mú

NUMBER 4: There a moo
NUMERO 4: Allá un mú

NUMBER 5: Everywhere a
NUMERO 5: En todas partes un

NUMBER 6: Moo-moo.
NUMERO 6: Mú-mú.

NUMBER 1: Old MacDonald
NUMERO 1: El Viejo MacDonald

NUMBER 2: Had a farm
NUMERO 2: Tenía una finca

NUMBER 3: E-I-E-I-O
NUMERO 3: E-I-E-I-O

NUMBER 4: And on this farm
NUMERO 4: Y en esta finca

NUMBER 5: He had some donkeys
NUMERO 5: Él tenía algunos burros

NUMBER 6: E-I-E-I-O

NUMERO 6: E-I-E-I-O

NUMBER 1: With a hee-haw here

NUMERO 1: Con un hi-ha aquí

NUMBER 2: And a hee-haw there

NUMERO 2: Y un hi-ha allá

NUMBER 3: Here a hee

NUMERO 3: Aquí un hi

NUMBER 4: There a haw

NUMERO 4: Allá un ha

NUMBER 5: Everywhere a

NUMERO 5: En todas partes un

NUMBER 6: Hee-haw.

NUMERO 6: Hi-ha

NUMBER 1: Old MacDonald

NUMERO 1: El Viejo MacDonald

NUMBER 2: Had a farm

NUMERO 2: Tenía una finca

NUMBER 3: E-I-E-I-O

NUMERO 3: E-I-E-I-O

NUMBER 4: And on this farm

NUMERO 4: Y en esta finca

NUMBER 5: He had some pigs

NUMERO 5: Él tenía algunos cerdos

NUMBER 6: E-I-E-I-O

NUMERO 6: E-I-E-I-O

NUMBER 1: With an oink-oink here

NUMERO 1: Con un oink-oink aquí

NUMBER 2: And an oink-oink there

NUMERO 2: Y un oink-oink allá

NUMBER 3: Here a oink

NUMERO 3: Aquí un oink

NUMBER 4: There a oink

NUMERO 4: Allá un oink

NUMBER 5: Everywhere an

NUMERO 5: En todas partes un

NUMBER 6: Oink-oink.

NUMERO 6: Oink-oink

NUMBER 1: Old MacDonald

NUMERO 1: El Viejo MacDonald

NUMBER 2: Had a farm

NUMERO 2: Tenía una finca

NUMBER 3: E-I-E-I-O

NUMERO 3: E-I-E-I-O

NUMBER 4: And on this farm

NUMERO 4: Y en esta finca

NUMBER 5: He had some ducks

NUMERO 5: Él tenía algunos patos

NUMBER 6: E-I-E-I-O

NUMERO 6: E-I-E-I-O

NUMBER 1: With a quack-quack here

NUMERO 1: Con un quac-quac aquí

NUMBER 2: And a quack-quack there

NUMERO 2: Y un quac-quac allá

NUMBER 3: Here a quack

NUMERO 3: Aquí un quac

NUMBER 4: There a quack

NUMERO 4: Allá un quac

NUMBER 5: Everywhere a

NUMERO 5: En todas partes un

NUMBER 6: Quack-quack.

NUMERO 6: Quac-quac.

NUMBER 1: Old MacDonald

NUMERO 1: El Viejo MacDonald

NUMBER 2: Had a farm

NUMERO 2: Tenía una finca

ALL: E-I-E-I-O

TODOS: E-I-E-I-O

Twinkle, Twinkle Little Star

PRESENTATION SUGGESTIONS

The four characters can all be standing. If preferable, the "Star" can stand while the other characters can be placed on stools.

PROPS

There are no props necessary. You may wish to consider providing the "Star" with a flashlight or lantern of some sort.

DELIVERY

Sammy and Tammy should both talk in loud voices (as though they are yelling up into the sky). Both the narrator and the "Star" should use their "classroom voices."

ORIGINAL VERSION

Twinkle, twinkle, little star.
How I wonder what you are,
Up above the world so high,
Like a diamond in the sky.
Twinkle, twinkle, little star,
How I wonder what you are!

PHONEMIC AWARENESS ACTIVITY(IES)

1. After students have become familiar with the original version of this rhyme, say the first line for them and ask them to respond with the second line. Then change the word at the end of the first line and invite the students to respond with the second line. Repeat several times, each time replacing the word at the end of line 1 with one of the words below, and then saying the line aloud to be followed by the students responding with line 2 (tell students that some of the words are nonsense words).

car	bar	tar	far	lar
mar	var	gar	par	sar

2. Repeat the activity above using lines 3 and 4 in the rhyme. Each time, substitute the word at the end of line 3 with one of the following words (again, some words will be nonsense words).

bye	lie	my	vie	kie	tie
sigh	die	rye	gie	pie	

Twinkle, Twinkle Little Star

Titila, Titila Pequeña Estrella

STAGING: The "Star" should be in the far corner of the staging area. Sammy and Tammy should be standing in the middle of the staging area. The narrator may be seated or standing.

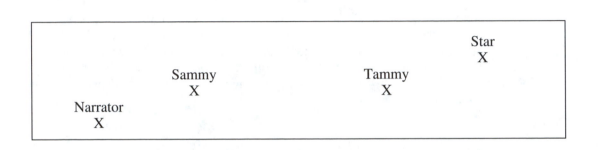

NARRATOR: Hello. Once there was a star. He didn't have a name. Everyone called him "Star" [turns to "Star"]. Hi, Star. One day the star said . . . .

NARRADOR(A): Hola. Una vez había una estrella. Que no tenía nombre. Todos la llamaban "Estrella" [volteandose a "Estrella"]. Hola, Estrella. Un día la estrella dijo . . . .

STAR: Hi, I'm a star. I'm up here. Up in the sky. I shine. I'm bright. That's what I do.

ESTRELLA: Hola, Yo soy una estrella. Estoy arriba. En lo alto del cielo. Yo brillo. Yo resplandezco. Eso es lo que hago.

NARRATOR: So, one day a boy and a girl saw the star.

NARRADOR(A): Entonces, un día un niño y una niña vieron la estrella.

SAMMY: Hey, look up there.

SAMMY: Oye, mira hacia arriba.

TAMMY: Where?

TAMMY: ¿Adónde?

SAMMY: Up there [pointing to "Star"].

SAMMY: Arriba [señalando a la "Estrella"].

TAMMY: Oh, yeah, now I see it.

TAMMY: Ah, sí, ahora la veo.

SAMMY: Yes, it's a star.

SAMMY: Sí, es una estrella.

TAMMY: Yes, and it is very bright.

TAMMY: Sí, y es muy resplandeciente.

SAMMY: Yes, and it shines a lot.

SAMMY: Sí, y brilla mucho.

TAMMY: What does a star do?

TAMMY: ¿Qué hace una estrella?

SAMMY: I don't know. Can we ask him?

SAMMY: Yo no sé. ¿Le podemos preguntar?

TAMMY: Let's ask him.

TAMMY: Vamos a preguntarle.

SAMMY: O.K. Hey, Mr. Star.

SAMMY: Está bien. Oiga, Señora Estrella.

From *Mother Goose Readers Theatre for Beginning Readers* by Anthony D. Fredericks. Westport, CT: Teacher Ideas Press. Copyright © 2007 by Anthony D. Fredericks.

STAR: Yes.

ESTRELLA: Sí.

SAMMY: What do you do?

SAMMY: ¿Qué hace usted?

STAR: Thanks for asking. I am in the sky. I am far away. I twinkle. I shine. And, I'm bright.

ESTRELLA: Gracias por preguntar. Estoy en el cielo. Estoy muy lejos. Yo titilo. Yo brillo. Y, resplandezco.

TAMMY: That's cool!

TAMMY: ¡Que chévere!

STAR: Yes, it is.

ESTRELLA: Sí, es chévere.

TAMMY: What else do you do?

TAMMY: ¿Qué más hace?

STAR: I make light.

ESTRELLA: Yo destello luz.

SAMMY: Yes, I can see. What else?

SAMMY: Sí, lo puedo ver. ¿Qué más?

STAR: I look like a diamond.

ESTRELLA: Yo luzco como un diamante.

TAMMY: I like diamonds. My mother has diamonds.

TAMMY: Me gustan los diamantes. Mi mamá tiene diamantes.

From *Mother Goose Readers Theatre for Beginning Readers* by Anthony D. Fredericks. Westport, CT: Teacher Ideas Press. Copyright © 2007 by Anthony D. Fredericks.

STAR:	Are they as bright as me?
ESTRELLA:	¿Son tan brillantes como yo?
TAMMY:	No. You are really bright!
TAMMY:	No. ¡Usted es muy brillante!
STAR:	Why, thank you.
ESTRELLA:	Pues, gracias.
TAMMY:	You're welcome.
TAMMY:	De nada.
SAMMY:	How long have you been there?
SAMMY:	¿Cuánto hace que está allí?
STAR:	I've been here for a long time.
ESTRELLA:	Yo he estado aquí por mucho tiempo.
TAMMY:	How long?
TAMMY:	¿Cuanto tiempo?
STAR:	Millions of years!
ESTRELLA:	¡Millones de años!
SAMMY:	Wow! That's a long time.
SAMMY:	¡Caramba! Eso es mucho tiempo.
STAR:	Yes, it is. I will be here for another million years.
ESTRELLA:	Sí, lo es. Yo estaré aquí por otros millónes de años.

From *Mother Goose Readers Theatre for Beginning Readers* by Anthony D. Fredericks. Westport, CT: Teacher Ideas Press. Copyright © 2007 by Anthony D. Fredericks.

TAMMY: You must be really old.

TAMMY: Usted debe ser muy vieja.

STAR: Yes, I am. But people still like me.

ESTRELLA: Sí, soy vieja. Pero todavía le gusto a la gente.

SAMMY: They like you because you are bright.

SAMMY: Les gusta porque usted es resplandeciente.

STAR: Yes, and people like to make wishes.

ESTRELLA: Sí, y a la gente le gusta pedir deseos.

TAMMY: What kind of wishes?

TAMMY: ¿Qué tipos de deseos?

STAR: People like to wish for horses. They wish for cars. And they wish for money.

ESTRELLA: A la gente le gusta pedir por caballos. Pedir por autos. Y pedir por dinero.

SAMMY: Why do they do that?

SAMMY: ¿Por qué lo hacen?

STAR: I don't know. Maybe they just want stuff.

ESTRELLA: Yo no sé. Quizás solo quieren cosas.

TAMMY: Well, I like you because you are so bright.

TAMMY: Bueno, usted a mi me gusta porque es resplandeciente.

STAR: Thank you, again.

ESTRELLA: Gracias, de nuevo.

From *Mother Goose Readers Theatre for Beginning Readers* by Anthony D. Fredericks. Westport, CT: Teacher Ideas Press. Copyright © 2007 by Anthony D. Fredericks.

TAMMY:	You're welcome, again.
TAMMY:	De nada.
NARRATOR:	So, look up. You can see lots of stars. Maybe you can make a wish.
NARRADOR(A):	Entonces, miren hacia arriba. Pueden ver muchas estrellas. Quizás puedan pedir un deseo.
STAR:	I hope to see you soon. Good-bye!
ESTRELLA:	Espero verlos pronto. ¡Adiós!

Humpty Dumpty

PRESENTATION SUGGESTIONS

This script uses the familiar Mother Goose rhyme embedded in another story. Be sure your students are familiar with the Big Bad Wolf character and some of the stories in which he appears (e.g., "Little Red Riding Hood," "The Three Little Pigs," etc.).

PROPS

No props are necessary for this production.

DELIVERY

The characters should all be having a comfortable and friendly conversation—similar to what they would have on the playground or during recess. The Big Bad Wolf should act confused and unsure of his role in the story.

ORIGINAL VERSION

Humpty Dumpty sat on a wall;
Humpty Dumpty had a great fall!
All the king's horses
And all the king's men
Couldn't put Humpty together again.

PHONEMIC AWARENESS ACTIVITY(IES)

1. Replace "Humpty Dumpty" with the names of students in the class and reread the rhyme out loud to students. For example, "Sally Rally sat on a wall. Sally Rally had a great fall . . . ." Or, "Tony Baloney sat on a wall. Tony Baloney had a great fall . . . ." Invite students to contribute imaginative names for each person in the room. Invite students to repeat the rhyme along with you for each new name.

2. After students are familiar with this Mother Goose rhyme, invite them to contribute their own rhymes. For example, say the first three lines and invite students to add a fourth line of their own choosing. ("Humpty Dumpty sat on a wall. Humpty Dumpty . . . . What sentence could we add to the end that would make this rhyme?")

Humpty Dumpty

STAGING: The characters may be seated on stools or chairs. They may also be standing or positioned at individual lecterns.

Girl 1	Girl 2	Boy 1	Boy 2	Big Bad Wolf
X	X	X	X	X

GIRL 1: Hello, Audience [waves to the audience].

GIRL 2: Yes, hello Audience [waves to audience].

BOY 1: We are happy to be here!

BOY 2: Yes, we have a funny story to share.

BIG BAD WOLF: Grumble, grumble, grumble

GIRL 1: Hey, why is the Big Bad Wolf in this story?

GIRL 2: I don't know. Do you know [points to Boy 1]?

BOY 1: I don't know. Do you know [points to Boy 2]?

BOY 2: I don't know why he is here. He sure looks strange.

BIG BAD WOLF: Yeah, why am I here? I think the author made a big mistake.

GIRL 1: What do you mean?

BIG BAD WOLF: I don't think the writer of this story is very smart.

GIRL 2: Yeah, you're right. Isn't this a story about a big egg?

BOY 1: Yes, it is. It's a story about a big egg, not a big bad wolf.

BIG BAD WOLF: Yeah, I don't get it. Maybe the author went to sleep when he was writing this story.

BOY 2: Yeah, I don't think the writer was paying attention.

BIG BAD WOLF: So, is it O.K. if I leave?

GIRL 1: I guess so.

GIRL 2: I think it's O.K.

BOY 1: What about the writer?

BIG BAD WOLF: I wouldn't listen to him any more. He doesn't know what he is doing.

BOY 2: I think you're right.

GIRL 1: So, I guess you can leave.

BIG BAD WOLF: I think I'll go over to another story.

GIRL 2: Which one?

BIG BAD WOLF: I think there's a story about some pigs. I think they try to build houses. One of the pigs isn't very smart.

BOY 1: Oh, you mean like the writer of this story.

BIG BAD WOLF: Yeah, just like the writer.

BOY 2: O.K., we'll see you later.

BIG BAD WOLF: Yeah. See you later. [The "Wolf" exits offstage.]

GIRL 1: Now, we can do our story. Is everybody ready?

ALL: Yes.

GIRL 1: Then, let's go. Humpty Dumpty . . .

GIRL 2: . . . sat on a wall.

BOY 1: Humpty Dumpty . . .

BOY 2: . . . had a great fall

GIRL 1: All the . . .

GIRL 2: . . . king's horses

BOY 1: And all . . .

BOY 2: . . . the king's men

GIRL 1: Couldn't . . .

From *Mother Goose Readers Theatre for Beginning Readers* by Anthony D. Fredericks. Westport, CT: Teacher Ideas Press. Copyright © 2007 by Anthony D. Fredericks.

GIRL 2: . . . put Humpty . . .

BOY 1: . . . together . . .

BOY 2: . . . again.

GIRL 1: Hey, that was very good.

GIRL 2: Yes, you're right.

BOY 1: And, you know what?

BOY 2: What?

BOY 1: We didn't need that old Big Bad Wolf.

GIRL 1: Yeah, we didn't need the wolf at all.

GIRL 2: I hope he found another story.

BOY 1: I hope he did, too.

BOY 2: I think he did. But I'm a little worried about those pigs.

Little Miss Muffet

PRESENTATION SUGGESTIONS

There are some unfamiliar words in this popular Mother Goose rhyme. However, this script provides students with the definitions for those words, so no vocabulary preparation is necessary beforehand. You may wish to tell students that this rhyme is more than 300 years old. There actually was a Miss Muffet (her first name was "Patience").

PROPS

A large pillow (for Miss Muffet). Optional: If several students have never tasted cottage cheese, you may wish to bring in small samples for them (please be aware of any dairy allergies).

DELIVERY

The narrators should all sound inquisitive, as should the Spider. Miss Muffet should sound "all knowing." The narrators should pause slightly after their reading of the original rhyme in the first part of the script.

ORIGINAL VERSION

Little Miss Muffet
Sat on a tuffet,
Eating her curds and whey.
There came a big spider,
Who sat down beside her
And frightened Miss Muffet away.

PHONEMIC AWARENESS ACTIVITY(IES)

1. After the students are familiar with this rhyme, ask them to listen to the following words: *muffet, sat, tuffet.* Point out that all of these words end in the same sound (/t/). Tell students that you want them to listen to the following words from the rhyme and tell you the sound at the end of each word:

    – miss /s/

    – on /n/

    – her /r/

    – came /m/

    – big /g/

    – spider /r/

    – down /n/

    – beside /d/

    – and /d/

Little Miss Muffet

STAGING: The three narrators may sit on tall stools or chairs in the rear of the staging area. The two main characters (Miss Muffet, Spider) should be in the middle of the staging area. Miss Muffet should be seated on a large pillow and the Spider on the floor.

Narrator 1 X	Narrator 2 X	Narrator 3 X
Miss Muffet X	Spider X	

NARRATOR 1: Little Miss Muffet

NARRATOR 2: Sat on a tuffet,

NARRATOR 3: Eating her curds and whey.

NARRATOR 1: There came a big spider,

NARRATOR 2: Who sat down beside her

NARRATOR 3: And frightened Miss Muffet away.

NARRATOR 1: Well, that's the story.

NARRATOR 2: Yes, a girl was eating . . . a spider came along . . .

NARRATOR 3: . . . she got scared . . .

NARRATOR 1: . . . and she ran away.

NARRATOR 2: There are some strange words in this story.

NARRATOR 3: Yes, you're right.

NARRATOR 1: Yeah, what is a tuffet?

MISS MUFFET: Maybe I can answer that.

NARRATOR 1: Well, thank you. And who are you?

MISS MUFFET: My name is Miss Muffet. I'm in the story.

NARRATOR 2: Oh, yes. I have heard about you.

From *Mother Goose Readers Theatre for Beginning Readers* by Anthony D. Fredericks. Westport, CT: Teacher Ideas Press. Copyright © 2007 by Anthony D. Fredericks.

MISS MUFFET: I hope so. You just told my story.

NARRATOR 3: So, what is a tuffet?

MISS MUFFET: Well, a tuffet is like a small chair.

NARRATOR 1: Is it like a small stool?

MISS MUFFET: Yes, it is also a low seat.

NARRATOR 2: So, it could be a very small chair.

MISS MUFFET: That's right.

SPIDER: Hey, now I have a question.

NARRATOR 3: What's that?

SPIDER: It says that she [points to Miss Muffet] eats some curds and whey.

NARRATOR 1: I know. You want to know what curds and whey are?

SPIDER: That's right. Every time we do the story, someone talks about curds and whey.

NARRATOR 2: I was wondering about that, too.

NARRATOR 3: So was I.

MISS MUFFET: Maybe I can help.

SPIDER: Please do.

MISS MUFFET: Well curds and whey is the same thing as cottage cheese.

NARRATOR 1: Oh, I get it. I eat that for lunch sometimes.

NARRATOR 2: So do I

NARRATOR 3: And, I do too. It's really very good.

SPIDER: So curds and whey must be an old way of saying cottage cheese.

MISS MUFFET: You're right.

From *Mother Goose Readers Theatre for Beginning Readers* by Anthony D. Fredericks. Westport, CT: Teacher Ideas Press. Copyright © 2007 by Anthony D. Fredericks.

SPIDER: Thank you, now I know. But I still have one question.

MISS MUFFET: What's that?

SPIDER: Why do you run away in the story?

MISS MUFFET: I guess I'm scared of you.

SPIDER: Why?

MISS MUFFET: I don't know. Maybe little girls are scared of spiders.

SPIDER: But, I'm very nice when you get to know me.

MISS MUFFET: You're right. You aren't scary at all.

SPIDER: So, can we be friends?

MISS MUFFET: I think we can.

SPIDER: And, maybe we can live happily ever after.

MISS MUFFET: Maybe we can.

ALL NARRATORS: The End!

From *Mother Goose Readers Theatre for Beginning Readers* by Anthony D. Fredericks. Westport, CT: Teacher Ideas Press. Copyright © 2007 by Anthony D. Fredericks.

The Cat and the Fiddle

PRESENTATION SUGGESTIONS

Students may benefit by seeing illustrations of this Mother Goose rhyme beforehand. There are many anthologies of Mother Goose rhymes (check in your school library) that contain illustrations of the characters and their respective actions. A familiarity with those actions helps set the stage for this production.

PROPS

No props are necessary.

DELIVERY

The characters should all read their lines in an upbeat and lighthearted way. This script explores some of the silliness in this popular rhyme, and the reading should convey a sense of fun and joy.

ORIGINAL VERSION

Hey, diddle, diddle,
The cat and the fiddle,
The cow jumped
Over the moon.
The little dog laughed
To see such sport,
And the dish ran away
With the spoon.

PHONEMIC AWARENESS ACTIVITY(IES)

1. Repeat the first two lines several times. Write the word *diddle* in large letters on the chalk-board. Tell your students that you are going to replace the first letter in that word with another letter. Say the new word for them and then invite them to repeat the first two lines using the new word. You may wish to use the following words, and then encourage students to invent their own:

biddle	middle	viddle
hiddle	niddle	widdle
jiddle	riddle	yiddle
kiddle	siddle	ziddle
liddle	tiddle	

The Cat and the Fiddle

STAGING: The narrator stands in back of or to the side of the characters. The characters may be standing or seated on tall stools.

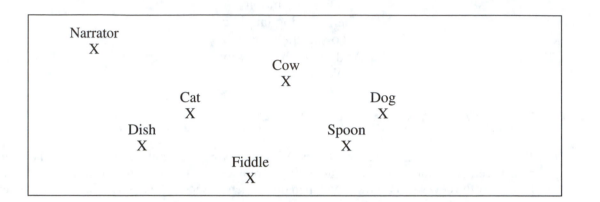

NARRATOR: Hey, diddle, diddle,

The cat and the fiddle,

The cow jumped

Over the moon.

The little dog laughed

To see such sport,

And the dish ran away

With the spoon.

COW: This is a good story.

CAT: Why do you say that?

COW: Because I get to jump over the moon.

DOG: How do you do that?

COW: Well, I guess I'm pretty strong.

DISH: You must be. I've never seen a cow jump that high before.

SPOON: I haven't either.

COW: Well, I've been doing a lot of exercises.

FIDDLE: You must have. I can't jump that high.

CAT: I can't either

DOG: But you [points to Cat] still can jump.

DISH: That's right. Cat is a very good jumper.

SPOON: Yes, I've seen him jump really high.

FIDDLE: But, in this story Cat doesn't jump.

COW: You're right

CAT: Yes, me and my friend Fiddle just sing.

DOG: Right. You sing "Hey, diddle, diddle."

DISH: I wish I could sing.

SPOON: Well, there's one thing you can do.

FIDDLE: That's right. You two [points to Dish and Spoon] get to run away.

COW: Where do you go?

CAT: Yeah, where do you two go?

DISH: I don't know.

SPOON: I don't know, either. The person who wrote the story didn't tell us.

DOG: Maybe you ran over to another story.

DISH: Maybe we did.

SPOON: And, maybe we didn't.

CAT: But, let's not forget our friend here [points to Dog].

FIDDLE: You're right. Our friend gets to laugh during the whole story.

DOG: Ha, ha, ha!

COW: I guess this is a really funny story.

CAT: Yes, it is. Look at all the funny things we do.

DISH: We do funny things . . .

SPOON: . . . and silly things . . .

FIDDLE: . . . and strange things!

COW: I guess that's why this is such a great story.

ALL: YEAH!!!

NARRATOR: Hey, diddle, diddle,

The cat and the fiddle,

The cow jumped

Over the moon.

The little dog laughed

To see such sport,

And the dish ran away

With the spoon.

Three Blind Mice

PRESENTATION SUGGESTIONS

This is a somewhat gruesome tale that originally chronicled a time in English history when people were burned at the stake for reading the Bible in English (so much for "merry old England"). However, this script takes a fun and lighthearted approach to this horrific time. Be sure to emphasize to students that everything in this script is symbolic and that it is just an imaginary story—a playful interaction between animals and humans.

PROPS

If possible, provide each of the mice with a set of sunglasses. Provide the Farmer's Wife with a plastic ruler (to symbolize the carving knife).

DELIVERY

The delivery should be fun and light. Note that the narrator gets frustrated with the mice at several spots during the story. The mice should be playful and silly.

ORIGINAL VERSION

Three blind mice,
Three blind mice.
See how they run!
See how they run!
They all ran after the farmer's wife,
Who cut off their tails with a carving knife,
Did you ever see such a thing in your life?
As three blind mice.

PHONEMIC AWARENESS ACTIVITY(IES)

1. Say one of the following word pairs to students. Tell the students that the first word in each pair is a word from the rhyme and that the second word in each pair is a word that you added. Invite students to suggest a third word that rhymes with the first two:

three—tree—_____	run—fun—_____
blind—mind—_____	ran—fan—_____
mice—rice—_____	cut—nut—_____
see—me—_____	seen—mean—_____
they—play—_____	life—knife—_____

Three Blind Mice

STAGING: The narrator should be seated on a tall stool or a chair to the side of the staging area. The other characters should all be standing. They may wish to move around the staging area as they say their lines.

```
Narrator
X
            Mouse 1        Mouse 2        Mouse 3
            X              X              X
                                              Farmer's Wife
                                              X
```

NARRATOR: Welcome to our story. This is an old story. It comes from England. It is the story of three mice . . . .

MOUSE 1: That's me.

MOUSE 2: And me.

MOUSE 3: And me, too.

NARRATOR: Anyway, as I was saying. There were these three mice [points to the three mice]. There is something else you must know about them. They are all blind.

MOUSE 1: Yes, we can't see.

MOUSE 2: Right, we can't see anything.

MOUSE 3: Yeah, like the narrator said . . . we're blind!

NARRATOR: [somewhat frustrated] Like I was saying . . . . There were these three mice. Well, as you know, mice like cheese.

MOUSE 1: Yes, we like cheese.

MOUSE 2: Yeah, we really like cheese.

MOUSE 3: Yum, Yum, C-H-E-E-S-E!

From *Mother Goose Readers Theatre for Beginning Readers* by Anthony D. Fredericks. Westport, CT: Teacher Ideas Press. Copyright © 2007 by Anthony D. Fredericks.

NARRATOR: [frustrated] Hey, you guys, I'm the narrator. All right. Please let me do my job and tell the story.

MOUSE 1: That's O.K. with me.

MOUSE 2: Me, too.

MOUSE 3: Me, too.

NARRATOR: Anyway, there were three mice. And they loved cheese. They also lived on a farm. They lived inside a farmhouse. Inside the house there was a mean old lady.

FARMER'S WIFE: Hey, wait a minute. I'm not mean. And, I'm not old.

NARRATOR: Well, that's what it says right here [points to script].

FARMER'S WIFE: Well, let's change that right now.

NARRATOR: What should we do?

FARMER'S WIFE: Well, let's make me young.

NARRATOR: O.K.

FARMER'S WIFE: And, let's make me pretty.

NARRATOR: O.K.

FARMER'S WIFE: So, now I'm the pretty young woman who lives in the farmhouse.

NARRATOR: O.K. So, inside the house was a pretty young lady. But sometimes she was angry. She was angry because the mice ate her cheese.

MOUSE 1: That's right, we ate her cheese.

MOUSE 2: Yum, Yum, cheese.

MOUSE 3: Yeah, yummy cheese.

NARRATOR: [frustrated] As I was saying . . . AGAIN! The mice would eat the pretty young lady's cheese. She was very mad when they did that. She was very, very mad.

FARMER'S WIFE: Yes, I was very, VERY mad!

NARRATOR: That's right. And, when she got mad she would chase the mice.

FARMER'S WIFE: Yes, I would chase those three blind mice [points] around the house. I didn't like them eating my cheese.

MOUSE 1: She was a fast runner.

MOUSE 2: Yes, she could run real fast.

MOUSE 3: She was a good runner.

NARRATOR: Well, one day she caught the mice. Then, she did something terrible.

MOUSE 1: Yes, it was terrible.

MOUSE 2: It was real terrible.

MOUSE 3: It was really bad.

FARMER'S WIFE: I had this knife [points to ruler in her hand]. I was cutting some bread. So, I caught the mice who were stealing my cheese. And, I cut off their tails.

MOUSE 1: Yes, she cut off our tails.

MOUSE 2: Yeah, that really hurt.

MOUSE 3: OUCH!!

NARRATOR: Well, there was a storyteller nearby. He heard the story of the three mice. He heard about the pretty young lady. So he made up a rhyme.

MOUSE 1: It was a story about us.

MOUSE 2: And, about the lady with the knife.

MOUSE 3: It's been around for a long time.

NARRATOR: That's right. So now our players [points to all the characters] will tell you the Mother Goose rhyme about the Three Blind Mice.

From *Mother Goose Readers Theatre for Beginning Readers* by Anthony D. Fredericks. Westport, CT: Teacher Ideas Press. Copyright © 2007 by Anthony D. Fredericks.

MOUSE 1: Three blind mice,

MOUSE 2: Three blind mice;

MOUSE 3: See how they run,

FARMER'S WIFE: See how they run!

MOUSE 1: They all ran after the farmer's wife,

MOUSE 2: Who cut off their tails with a carving knife.

MOUSE 3: Have you ever seen such a sight

FARMER'S WIFE: In your life as three blind mice?

NARRATOR: And that's our story. Thank you and good night!

From *Mother Goose Readers Theatre for Beginning Readers* by Anthony D. Fredericks. Westport, CT: Teacher Ideas Press. Copyright © 2007 by Anthony D. Fredericks.

One, Two,
Buckle My Shoe

PRESENTATION SUGGESTIONS

This should be a familiar Mother Goose rhyme for most children. You may wish to have students repeat the script a second time—immediately after the first telling. For the second go-round, invite students (the audience) to use different words that rhyme with "show," "door," "sticks," "gate," and "hen."

PROPS

No props are necessary for this script.

DELIVERY

The delivery should be quick and perky. Encourage students to keep the pace flowing smoothly.

ORIGINAL VERSION

One, two, buckle my shoe.
Three, four, knock at the door.
Five, six, pick up sticks.
Seven, eight, lay them straight.
Nine, ten, a good fat hen.

PHONEMIC AWARENESS ACTIVITY(IES)

1.   For lots of silliness (and just plain fun), invite students to suggest new rhyming sentences for each pair of numbers. For example:

– One, two, eat some stew;

– Three, four, daddy can snore;

– Five, six, my dog eats sticks;

– Seven, eight, my nose is straight;

– Nine, ten, let's do it again.

You may want to post some of these silly sentences on a classroom bulletin board.

One, Two, Buckle My Shoe

Uno, Dos, Abrocha Mi Zapato

STAGING: The characters may be seated on chairs or stools. The narrators should be off to the side and may be at individual podiums.

	Tim	Kim	Roy	Joy
	X	X	X	X
Narrator 1	Narrator 2			
X	X			

NARRATOR 1: This is a counting story.

NARRADOR(A) 1: Este es un cuento de contar.

NARRATOR 2: We will use numbers.

NARRADOR(A) 2: Nosotros usarémos los números.

NARRATOR 1: And we will use words that rhyme.

NARRADOR(A) 1: Y nosotros usarémos palabras que rimen.

NARRATOR 2: Maybe you [points to audience] can help us.

NARRADOR(A) 2: Tal vez ustedes [señalando a la audiencia] nos puedan ayudar.

NARRATOR 1: So listen carefully . . .

NARRADOR(A) 1: Entonces escuchen cuidadosamente . . .

NARRATOR 2: . . . and we will tell you a story.

NARRADOR(A) 2: . . . y nosotros les contarémos un cuento.

From *Mother Goose Readers Theatre for Beginning Readers* by Anthony D. Fredericks. Westport, CT: Teacher Ideas Press. Copyright © 2007 by Anthony D. Fredericks.

NARRATOR 1: Here goes.

NARRADOR(A) 1: Aquí va.

TIM: One, two,

TIM: Uno, dos,

KIM: Buckle my shoe.

KIM: Abrocha mi zapato.

ROY: Three, four,

ROY: Tres, cuatro,

JOY: Knock at the door.

JOY: Toca a la puerta.

TIM: Five, six,

TIM: Cinco, seis,

KIM: Pick up sticks

KIM: Recoge las ramitas

ROY: Seven, eight,

ROY: Siete, ocho,

JOY: Lay them straight.

JOY: Pon las derechas.

TIM: Nine, ten,

TIM: Nueve, diez,

KIM: A good fat hen.

KIM: Una buena gallina gorda.

NARRATOR 2: O.K. [points to audience], are you ready?

NARRADOR(A) 2: ¿Está bien [señalando a la audiencia], están listos?

AUDIENCE: YES!

AUDIENCIA: ¡SÍ!

NARRATOR 1: One person [points to four characters] will say the first line . . .

NARRADOR(A) 1: Una persona [señalando a los cuatro personajes] dirá la primera linea . . .

NARRATOR 2: Then, a second person will begin the next line . . .

NARRADOR(A) 2: Luego, una segunda persona empezará la proxima linea . . .

NARRATOR 1: . . . and you [points to audience] will say the last word.

NARRADOR(A) 1: . . . y ustedes [señalando a la audiencia] dirán la última palabra.

NARRATOR 2: Remember, the last word . . .

NARRADOR(A) 2: Recuerden, la última palabra . . .

NARRATOR 1: . . . must rhyme with the word in the first sentence.

NARRADOR(A) 1: . . . deberá rimar con la palabra en la primera oración.

NARRATOR 2: O.K.? Here we go.

NARRADOR(A) 2: ¿Está bien? Aquí vamos.

TIM: One, two,

TIM: Uno, dos,

From *Mother Goose Readers Theatre for Beginning Readers* by Anthony D. Fredericks. Westport, CT: Teacher Ideas Press. Copyright © 2007 by Anthony D. Fredericks.

KIM: Buckle my _____.

KIM: Abrocha mi _____.

AUDIENCE: [The audience may use the word "shoe" or any other word that rhymes with "two."]

AUDIENCIA: [La audiencia puede usar la palabra "zapato" o cualquier otra palabra que rime con "dos."]

ROY: Three, four,

ROY: Tres, cuatro,

JOY: Knock at the _____.

JOY: Toca la _____.

AUDIENCE: [The audience may use any word that rhymes with "four."]

AUDIENCIA: [La audiencia puede usar cualquier palabra que rime con "cuatro."]

TIM: Five, six,

TIM: Cinco, seis,

KIM: Pick up _____.

KIM: Recoge _____.

AUDIENCE: [The audience may use any word that rhymes with "six."]

AUDIENCIA: [La audiencia puede usar cualquier palabra que rime con "seis."]

ROY: Seven, eight

ROY: Siete, ocho

JOY: Lay them _____.

JOY: Pon los _____.

AUDIENCE: [The audience may use any word that rhymes with "eight."]

AUDIENCIA: [La audiencia puede usar cualquier palabra que rime con "ocho."]

TIM: Nine, ten,

TIM: Nueve, diez,

KIM: A good fat _____.

KIM: Un bueno _____ gordo.

AUDIENCE: [The audience may use any word that rhymes with "ten."]

AUDIENCIA: [La audiencia puede usar cualquier palabra que rime con "diez."]

NARRATOR 1: You all [points to audience] did a very good job.

NARRADOR(A) 1: Ustedes [señalando a la audiencia] hicieron un buen trabajo.

NARRATOR 2: And you [points to players) did a very good job, too.

NARRADOR(A) 2: Y ustedes [señalando a los personajes] hicieron un buen trabajo, también.

AUDIENCE: YEAH!

AUDIENCIA: ¡SÍ!

PLAYERS: YEAH!

PERSONAJES: ¡SÍ!

From *Mother Goose Readers Theatre for Beginning Readers* by Anthony D. Fredericks. Westport, CT: Teacher Ideas Press. Copyright © 2007 by Anthony D. Fredericks.

Pat-a-Cake

PRESENTATION SUGGESTIONS

Point out to students that this script has a few parts for the audience. Members of the audience will have to listen carefully to the players. If they do, they will be able to present or repeat their parts without any difficulty.

PROPS

No props are necessary for this script. You may, however, wish to put a cupcake on a table in the middle of the five characters. Each of the characters can then point to the cupcake as they say their parts.

DELIVERY

The delivery should be smooth. Characters may wish to practice their parts before performing them in front of a group.

ORIGINAL VERSION

Pat-a-cake, pat-a-cake,
Baker's man!
Bake me a cake,
As fast as you can.
Pat it and prick it,
And mark it with a B.
Put it in the oven
For Baby and me.

PHONEMIC AWARENESS ACTIVITY(IES)

1. Repeat this rhyme several times, each time changing the letter at the end of line 6 to each of the following:

   C   D   E   G   P   T   V   Z

   Invite students to repeat the sixth line each time you substitute a new letter.

2. Repeat the activity above and change the letter at the end of line 6 to each of the following letters. Each time, complete the last two lines of the rhyme and invite students to suggest an appropriate rhyming word. For example:

   A (kay, may, lay, say)
   I (pie, sky, rye, tie)
   O (crow, moe, flow, bow, toe)
   U (you, crew, lou, stew)

Pat-a-Cake

STAGING: The characters may be seated in a semicircle on tall stools or on chairs. There is no narrator for this script.

```
                          C
                          X
              B                       D
              X                       X
    A                                           E
    X                                           X
```

A: Pat-a-cake,

B: Pat-a-cake

C: Baker's man!

D: Bake me a cake,

E: As fast as you can.

A: Pat it,

B: And prick it,

C: And mark it with a B.

D: Put it in the oven

E: For baby and me.

A: This time, you [points to B] start. O.K.

B: O.K. Here goes. Pat-a-cake,

C: Pat-a-cake

D: Baker's man!

E: Bake me a cake,

A: As fast as you can.

B: Pat it,

C: And prick it,

D: And mark it with a B.

E: Put it in the oven

A: For baby and me.

B: Hey, that was fun. This time, you [points to C] start. O.K.?

C: O.K. Here goes. Pat-a-cake,

D: Pat-a-cake

E: Baker's man!

A: Bake me a cake,

B: As fast as you can.

C: Pat it,

D: And prick it,

E: And mark it with a B.

A: Put it in the oven

B: For baby and me.

C: That was neat. Let's do it one more time!

D: O.K. Here goes. Pat-a-cake,

E: Pat-a-cake

A: Baker's man!

B: Bake me a cake,

C: As fast as you can.

D: Pat it,

E: And prick it,

A: And mark it with a B.

From *Mother Goose Readers Theatre for Beginning Readers* by Anthony D. Fredericks. Westport, CT: Teacher Ideas Press. Copyright © 2007 by Anthony D. Fredericks.

B: Put it in the oven

C: For baby and me.

D: Now, you [points to audience] can help us out. O.K.?

AUDIENCE: O.K.

E: Here we go. Pat-a-cake,

AUDIENCE: Pat-a-cake,

A: Baker's man!

AUDIENCE: Bake me a cake,

B: As fast as you can.

AUDIENCE: Pat it,

C: And prick it,

AUDIENCE: And mark it with a B.

D: Put it in the oven

AUDIENCE: For baby and me.

E: For baby and me!

ALL: For baby and me!

Hickory, Dickory Dock

PRESENTATION SUGGESTIONS

Inform students that this is a nonsense rhyme. It's silly and doesn't have any real purpose other than to show the fun that can be had with words and language. With only four parts, the script can be repeated several times with several different children taking over each part.

PROPS

You may wish to have a photograph or sketch of a grandfather clock posted on a wall in back of the players. If preferred, you may wish to put a set of construction paper ears on the "mouse."

DELIVERY

Students may wish to slow down the delivery of this script due to the alliterative nature of the words. After sufficient practice, they can speed up the process.

ORIGINAL VERSION

Hickory, dickory, dock,
The mouse ran up the clock.
The clock struck one,
The mouse ran down,
Hickory, dickory, dock.

PHONEMIC AWARENESS ACTIVITY(IES)

1. Encourage students to suggest new alliterative letters for each of the first three words and last three words of the rhyme. For example: "Hickory, hickory, hock . . . " or "Sickory, sickory, sock . . . ."

2. Invite students to substitute a new consonant sound in the middle of each of the first three words and last three words in the rhyme. For example: "Himmory, dimmory, domm . . . " or "Hittory, dittory, dott . . . ."

Hickory, Dickory, Dock

Jicori, Dicori, Doc

STAGING: There is no narrator for this script. The "mouse" should be standing and can move around the staging area. The other characters may be seated on chairs or stools.

	Person 1 X	Person 2 X	Person 3 X
Mouse X			

MOUSE: Hi, I'm a mouse.

RATÓN: Hola, yo soy un ratón.

PERSON 1: You look cute.

PERSONA 1: Me pareces lindo.

MOUSE: Why, thank you.

RATÓN: Pues, gracias.

PERSON 2: You look fast.

PERSONA 2: Me pareces rápido.

MOUSE: Yes, I am. I can run fast.

RATÓN: Sí, lo soy. Puedo correr rápido.

PERSON 3: And, you look smart.

PERSONA 3: Y, me pareces listo.

MOUSE: Yes, I am smart.

RATÓN: Sí, yo soy listo.

From *Mother Goose Readers Theatre for Beginning Readers* by Anthony D. Fredericks. Westport, CT: Teacher Ideas Press. Copyright © 2007 by Anthony D. Fredericks.

PERSON 1: So, let's tell a story about you.

PERSONA 1: Entonces, vamos a contar un cuento sobre ti.

PERSON 2: Yes, a story.

PERSONA 2: Sí, un cuento.

PERSON 3: It's a story called "Hickory, Dickory, Dock."

PERSONA 3: Es un cuento llamado "Jicori, Dicori, Doc."

MOUSE: I'm ready.

RATÓN: Estoy listo.

PERSON 1: Hickory, Dickory

PERSONA 1: Jicori, Dicori

PERSON 2: Dock

PERSONA 2: Doc

PERSON 3: The Mouse

PERSONA 3: El Ratón

MOUSE: That's me!

RATÓN: ¡Ese soy yo!

PERSON 1: Ran up the clock.

PERSONA 1: Se subió al reloj.

PERSON 2: The clock struck one.

PERSONA 2: El reloj marcó la una.

PERSON 3: The mouse ran down

PERSONA 3: El ratón se bajó

MOUSE: That's me, again.

RATÓN: Ese soy yo, otra vez.

PERSON 1: Hickory,

PERSONA 1: Jicori,

PERSON 2: Dickory,

PERSONA 2: Dicori,

PERSON 3: Dock.

PERSONA 3: Doc.

MOUSE: I don't like loud sounds.

RATÓN: No me gustan los ruidos altos.

PERSON 1: He doesn't like loud sounds.

PERSONA 1: A él no le gustan los ruidos altos.

PERSON 2: Like a loud clock . . .

PERSONA 2: Como el ruidoso reloj . . .

PERSON 3: Or a Dickory, Dock!

PERSONA 3: ¡O un Dicori, Doc!

MOUSE: That's right. A clock is loud. But, what is a Dickory, Dock?

RATÓN: Así es. Un reloj es ruidoso. ¿Pero, qué es un Dicori, Doc?

PERSON 1: I don't know!

PERSONA 1: ¡Yo no sé!

PERSON 2: I don't know!

PERSONA 2: ¡Yo no sé!

PERSON 3: I don't know!

PERSONA 3: ¡Yo no sé!

MOUSE: HMMMM. That's funny. I know what a clock is. But, I don't know what a "Dickory Dock" is.

RATÓN: HMMMM. Eso es gracioso. Yo sé que es un reloj. Pero, no sé que es un "Dicori Doc".

PERSON 1: It's a funny word.

PERSONA 1: Es una palabra curiosa.

PERSON 2: Yes, it's a real funny word.

PERSONA 2: Sí, es una palabra realmente curiosa.

PERSON 3: Yes, It's funny. But I don't know what it means.

PERSONA 3: Sí, es curiosa. Pero yo no sé que significa.

MOUSE: Well, that's O.K. Let's Do it again.

RATÓN: Bueno, está bien. Vamos a hacerlo otra vez.

PERSON 1: O.K.

PERSONA 1: Está bien.

PERSON 2: O.K.

PERSONA 2: Está bien.

PERSON 3: O.K., here goes.

PERSONA 1: Está bien, aquí vamos.

PERSON 1: Hickory, Dickory

PERSONA 1: Jicori, Dicori

PERSON 2: Dock

PERSONA 2: Doc

PERSON 3: The Mouse

PERSONA 3: El Ratón

MOUSE: That's me!

RATÓN: ¡Ese soy yo!

PERSON 1: Ran up the clock.

PERSONA 1: Se subió al reloj.

PERSON 2: The clock struck one.

PERSONA 2: El reloj marcó la una.

PERSON 3: The mouse ran down

PERSONA 3: El ratón se bajó

MOUSE: That's me, again.

RATÓN: Ese soy yo, otra vez.

PERSON 1: Hickory,

PERSONA 1: Jicori,

PERSON 2: Dickory,

PERSONA 2: Dicori,

PERSON 3: Dock.

PERSONA 3: Doc.

There Was an Old Woman

PRESENTATION SUGGESTIONS

Near the end of this script the characters will all need to read their parts together. You may wish to have students practice reading in unison before performing this play.

PROPS

You may wish to place an old boot (one of yours or one obtained at your local Salvation Army or Goodwill store) on a table in front of all the characters.

DELIVERY

The characters ask many questions throughout this script. Be sure students use their "question-asking" voices when posing a query.

ORIGINAL VERSION

There was an old woman
Who lived in a shoe.
She had so many children,
She didn't know what to do.
She gave them some broth
Without any bread.
She kissed them all sweetly
And sent them to bed.

PHONEMIC AWARENESS ACTIVITY(IES)

1. After students are familiar with this Mother Goose rhyme, tell them that you will say the first two lines of the rhyme to them, but you will change the word at the end of line 2. You'll then say the third line and the first word of the fourth line—inviting them to complete the fourth line with something that will rhyme with the new word inserted into line 2. You may wish to share the examples below:

There was an old woman
Who lived in a *store*
She had so many children
She didn't want *more*.

There was an old woman
Who lived in a *tree*
She had so many children
More than one hundred *three*.

This activity works best if you keep it fun and silly. Here are some additional substitutions for the last word in line 2:

hat   sock   dress   car   train   store   box   shirt

There Was an Old Woman

STAGING: The narrator should stand off to one side of the staging area. The characters may be seated on chairs or tall stools.

	Number 1	Number 2	Number 3	Number 4
	X	X	X	X
Narrator				
X				

NARRATOR: There was an old woman . . . .

NUMBER 1: So, there was this old person.

NARRATOR: Yes, she was a very old lady.

NUMBER 2: What did she do?

NARRATOR: Well she lived in a shoe.

NUMBER 3: Why did she live in a shoe?

NARRATOR: I don't know!

NUMBER 4: That's strange—an old lady who lives in an old shoe.

NARRATOR: Yes, I know.

NUMBER 1: How did she get into the shoe?

NUMBER 2: A shoe can be really stinky.

NARRATOR: You're right. I just don't know.

NUMBER 3: Why would she live in a stinky shoe?

NUMBER 4: Maybe she didn't have a house.

NUMBER 1: Maybe she didn't have an apartment.

NUMBER 2: Maybe she didn't even have a tent.

NARRATOR: You could all be right.

NUMBER 3: Well, tell us more about this old lady.

NARRATOR: Well she had a lot of children.

NUMBER 4: How many children did she have?

NARRATOR: I don't know. I'm just telling the story.

NUMBER 1: Maybe she had a million children.

NUMBER 2: Wow! That would be a lot of kids!

NUMBER 3: Yeah, that would be a lot of brothers . . .

NUMBER 4: . . . and a lot of sisters!

NUMBER 1: I don't think I would want all those brothers . . .

NUMBER 2: . . . or sisters.

NUMBER 3: Well, tell us more.

NARRATOR: The old lady didn't know what to do with all those children.

NUMBER 4: I wouldn't know what to do.

NUMBER 1: I wouldn't know what to do.

NUMBER 2: Me, too.

NUMBER 3: She must have done something.

NARRATOR: She gave them some broth.

NUMBER 4: What is broth?

NARRATOR: It's just like soup. But there are no vegetables.

NUMBER 1: That's O.K. I don't like vegetables.

NUMBER 2: Then, you might like broth.

NUMBER 3: So, what did she do then?

NARRATOR: She didn't give them any bread.

NUMBER 4: Why was that?

NARRATOR: Because she didn't have any.

NUMBER 1: O.K. Then what?

NARRATOR: She sent them all to bed.

NUMBER 2: They must have been very tired . . .

NUMBER 3: . . . and very hungry.

NUMBER 4: She was tired and hungry, too.

NUMBER 1: I think you're right.

NUMBER 2: This isn't a happy story.

NUMBER 3: No, it's not.

NUMBER 4: But, let's hear the whole story . . .

NUMBER 1: . . . about the old woman . . .

NUMBER 2: . . . and all her kids . . .

NUMBER 3: . . . and what they ate . . .

NUMBER 4: . . . and how they all went to bed.

NARRATOR: O.K., I'll start and you all [points to characters] can help me out.

ALL: O.K.

NARRATOR: Here we go! There was an old woman

ALL: Who lived in a shoe,

NARRATOR: She had so many children,

ALL: She didn't know what to do.

NARRATOR: She gave them some broth

ALL: Without any bread.

NARRATOR: She kissed them all sweetly

ALL: And sent them to bed.

NARRATOR: You did a great job. Thank you very much.

ALL: You're welcome.

Little Jack Horner

PRESENTATION SUGGESTIONS

You may wish to share the Mother Goose rhyme with your students beforehand (particularly if there are several individuals not familiar with this rhyme). Let students know that a story has been built around the rhyme to add some interest.

PROPS

No props are necessary. However, if you can get a make-believe pie (or even a pie plate), that would add to the story's effect.

DELIVERY

The delivery should be slow and measured (this script does not require a rapid pace). Encourage the characters to speak to each other (rather than into their scripts).

ORIGINAL VERSION

Little Jack Horner
Sat in a corner
Eating his Christmas pie.
He stuck in his thumb,
Pulled out a plum,
And said, "What a good boy am I!"

PHONEMIC AWARENESS ACTIVITY(IES)

1.   Repeat the first five lines of the rhyme for your students, but change the body part at the end of line 4 (see samples below). Invite students to suggest a rhyming word for the end of line 5. For example:

- Leg: keg, peg
- Head: sled, bread
- Hand: band, land
- Arm: charm, farm
- Nose: hose, rose, toes
- Chest: best, rest, nest

Little Jack Horner

STAGING: The characters may be seated on stools or may be standing. Note that this script does not have a narrator.

Cat	Dog	Mouse	
X	X	X	
			Jack
			X

CAT: Hey, look, there's Jack.

DOG: What is he doing?

MOUSE: I don't know. Let's ask him. Hey, Jack. What are you doing?

JACK: Oh, nothing. I'm just walking around.

CAT: You look lost.

DOG: Yeah, you look lost.

MOUSE: Hey, Jack, are you lost?

JACK: No, I'm not lost. I'm just hungry.

CAT: Did you have any breakfast?

JACK: No.

DOG: Did you have any lunch?

JACK: No.

MOUSE: Did you have any dinner?

JACK: No.

CAT: Wow, you must be really hungry.

DOG: Yeah, you must be very hungry.

MOUSE: Hmmm, I wonder how we can help you.

JACK: I don't know. But I'm really really hungry.

CAT: I wonder if someone could give us some food.

DOG: That would be a good idea.

MOUSE: But, who would give us some food?

CAT: Let's look around.

DOG: Hey, look over there [points].

MOUSE: Hey, look at that. It's a pie. Somebody left it outside.

JACK: Boy, that sure looks good. What kind of pie is it?

CAT: It looks like a cherry pie.

DOG: No, it looks like a berry pie.

MOUSE: I think you are wrong. I think it's a plum pie.

CAT: How do you know?

DOG: Yeah, how do you know?

MOUSE: Well, it smells like a plum pie.

JACK: I know how I could find out.

CAT: How?

DOG: How?

MOUSE: Yeah, how?

JACK: Well, I could stick my thumb in the pie.

CAT: What would that do?

DOG: Yeah, what would that do?

MOUSE: What do you think you would find?

JACK: Well, if I found a plum, then I would know what kind of pie it was.

[Jack sits down and pretends to stick his thumb into a plum pie.]

CAT: I guess that means we should finish this story.

DOG: Yeah, I guess we should finish this story.

MOUSE: I think you're right. So, here goes.

CAT: Little Jack Horner

DOG: Sat in a corner

MOUSE: Eating his Christmas pie;

CAT: He put in his thumb,

DOG: And pulled out a plum,

MOUSE: And cried, "What a good boy am I!"

JACK: The End.

Rub-a-Dub-Dub

PRESENTATION SUGGESTIONS

This particular English rhyme has a naughty genesis (see "Interesting Facts about Mother Goose" at the end of this book). Nevertheless, for children it is a playful and silly story about three men who just happen to climb into a big tub for a journey across water. Their reasons for sailing in a tub are never known, but that just adds to the silliness. Keep the emphasis on fun and frivolity for this script.

PROPS

If you can obtain a large tub, you may wish to place it in the center of the staging area. This is optional, however.

DELIVERY

The Candlestick Maker should deliver his lines in a sing-song manner. The Butcher and Baker should deliver their lines with a somewhat puzzled expression on their faces. The narrator should be the "straight man" in this script.

ORIGINAL VERSION

Rub-a-dub-dub,
Three men in a tub,
And how do you think they got there?
The butcher, the baker, the candlestick maker,
They all jumped out of a rotten potato,
'Twas enough to make a man stare.

PHONEMIC AWARENESS ACTIVITY(IES)

1. You may wish to create a chant with students using selected words from the rhyme. For example:

It begins with /r/
And ends with /ub/.
Put them together
And they say _____ (rub)

Invite students to blend the sounds together and chorus the correct answer. Repeat the chant several times using some of the following words from the rhyme:

dub: /d/ /ub/
three: /th/ /ree/
tub: /t/ /ub/
think: /th/ /ink/
they: /th/ /ey/
There: /th/ /ere/

Rub-a-Dub-Dub

STAGING: The narrator should be placed in the rear of the staging area. She or he may sit on a tall stool or be standing in front of a music stand or lectern. The other characters should all be standing in the middle of the staging area.

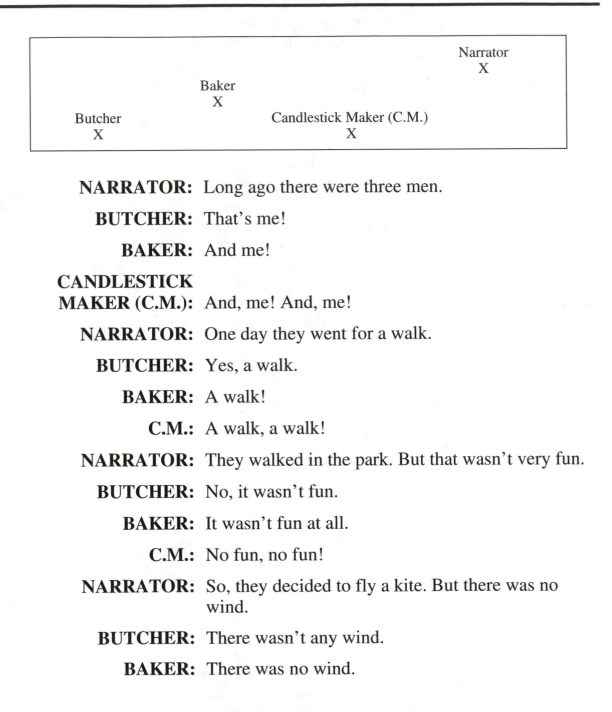

```
                                                      Narrator
                                                         X

                        Baker
                          X
        Butcher                      Candlestick Maker (C.M.)
           X                                  X
```

NARRATOR: Long ago there were three men.

BUTCHER: That's me!

BAKER: And me!

CANDLESTICK MAKER (C.M.): And, me! And, me!

NARRATOR: One day they went for a walk.

BUTCHER: Yes, a walk.

BAKER: A walk!

C.M.: A walk, a walk!

NARRATOR: They walked in the park. But that wasn't very fun.

BUTCHER: No, it wasn't fun.

BAKER: It wasn't fun at all.

C.M.: No fun, no fun!

NARRATOR: So, they decided to fly a kite. But there was no wind.

BUTCHER: There wasn't any wind.

BAKER: There was no wind.

C.M.: No wind, no wind.

NARRATOR: So, then they went on the swings. But the swings were broken.

BUTCHER: They were broken.

BAKER: They wouldn't work.

C.M.: Not working. Not working.

NARRATOR: So they thought some more. They decided to climb a tree.

BUTCHER: Yes, climb a tree.

BAKER: We can climb a tree.

C.M.: A tree. A tree.

NARRATOR: But, the tree was too high. "What shall we do?" they asked.

BUTCHER: Yes, what shall we do?

BAKER: What will we do?

C.M.: To do. To do.

NARRATOR: So they decided to row a boat. They decided to row a boat across the lake.

BUTCHER: Yes, let's row a boat.

BAKER: We can row a boat.

C.M.: A boat. A boat.

NARRATOR: But there was no boat. All they could find was an old tub.

BUTCHER: All we could find was a tub.

BAKER: We found a tub.

C.M.: A tub. A tub.

NARRATOR: So they said, "Let's try the tub. It should be fine."

BUTCHER: That's what we said.

BAKER: Yes, that's what we said.

C.M.: We said. We said.

NARRATOR: So, they all climbed into the tub. They floated out on the lake.

BUTCHER: We went out on the lake.

BAKER: Way out on the lake.

C.M.: The lake. The lake.

NARRATOR: I don't know what happened after that. They might still be there.

BUTCHER: Yes, we might still be there.

BAKER: We could still be on the lake.

C.M.: The lake. The lake.

NARRATOR: But, that's not the end. There is a rhyme that goes with this story. It's about these three men [points to the characters].

BUTCHER: It's about me, the butcher.

BAKER: And me, the baker.

C.M.: [points to self] Candlestick maker. Candlestick maker.

NARRATOR: And, here's that story.

BUTCHER: Rub-a-dub-dub

BAKER: Three men in a tub,

C.M.: And how do you think they got there?

BUTCHER: The butcher [points to self],

BAKER: The baker [points to self],

C.M.: The candlestick maker [points to self],

BUTCHER: They all

BAKER: Jumped out

 From *Mother Goose Readers Theatre for Beginning Readers* by Anthony D. Fredericks. Westport, CT: Teacher Ideas Press. Copyright © 2007 by Anthony D. Fredericks.

C.M.: Of a rotten potato,

NARRATOR: 'Twas enough to make a man stare.

ALL: The end.

C.M.: The end. The end!

PART II

READING LEVEL, SECOND GRADE

Baa, Baa, Black Sheep

PRESENTATION SUGGESTIONS

The Mother Goose rhyme is part of a larger script. You may wish to explain to students the meaning of the word "dame" (older woman) before a presentation. Depending on the background knowledge of your students, it may be necessary to explain that wool is the white fluffy stuff on sheep.

PROPS

You may wish to have a large grocery bag filled with scraps of paper and taped closed. The bag may be on the floor in front of the characters.

DELIVERY

"Sally" should have a quizzical expression on her face. The narrator should keep the pace of the story moving at a good clip.

ORIGINAL VERSION

Baa, baa, black sheep,
Have you any wool?
Yes, sir, yes, sir,
Three bags full:
One for the master,
One for the dame,
And one for the little boy
Who lives down the lane.

COMPREHENSION ACTIVITY(IES)

1.   Model for students some of the questions you would ask yourself as you read this book. Do a think-aloud for students using some of the following examples:

   – "Do I have any questions about the title before I read?"

   – "What do I like about the title?"

   – "What can I do if I don't understand something?"

   – "Am I enjoying the story so far?"

   – "Can I retell this story to someone else?"

   – "Would I want to read another Mother Goose rhyme like this?"

   As you do an initial read-aloud, slip some of the questions above into the storytelling. Pause each time and allow students to "see inside your head" as you model each question and as you think about how you might respond to each one. For example, if you asked yourself (in a talk-aloud), "What can I do if I don't understand something?", you could make up the following response: "Well, I guess if I didn't understand something, I could continue reading and hope that the author gives me some new information. Or maybe, I could ask a friend to help me figure out what is going on in the story." The scenarios don't have to be long, just illustrative of the thinking you might do as you ask and answer your own questions.

Baa, Baa, Black Sheep

Ba, Ba, Oveja Negra

STAGING: The characters should be standing. They may hold the scripts in their hands or the scripts may be placed on music stands placed in front of each character.

Narrator X				
	Sally X			
		Sarah X		
			Seth X	

NARRATOR: Once upon a time . . .

NARRADOR(A): Una vez había . . .

SALLY: There was a boy.

SALLY: Un niño.

NARRATOR: Hey, wait a minute.

NARRADOR(A): Oye, espera un minuto.

SALLY: What?

SALLY: ¿Qué?

NARRATOR: I'm the narrator. I should tell the story.

NARRADOR(A): Yo soy el narrador. Yo debo contar el cuento.

SALLY: O.K. you're right.

SALLY: Está bien, tienes razón.

From *Mother Goose Readers Theatre for Beginning Readers* by Anthony D. Fredericks. Westport, CT: Teacher Ideas Press. Copyright © 2007 by Anthony D. Fredericks.

SARAH: Yes, let's let the narrator tell the story.

SARA: Sí, vamos a permitirle al narrador contar el cuento.

SETH: Yes, I agree. The narrator should tell the story.

SETH: Sí, estoy de acuerdo. El narrador debe contar el cuento.

SALLY: Then what do we do?

SALLY: ¿Qué harémos luego?

SARAH: We listen.

SARA: Nosotros escucharémos.

SETH: And, we help the narrator.

SETH: Y, ayudarémos al narrador.

SALLY: How do we help?

SALLY: ¿Cómo ayudarémos?

SARAH: We have things to say.

SARA: Nosotros tenemos cosas que decir.

SALLY: When do we say them?

SALLY: ¿Cuándo decirlas?

SETH: When the narrator is done talking.

SETH: Cuando el narrador termine de hablar.

SALLY: O.K.

SALLY: Está bien.

NARRATOR: Can I start now?

NARRADOR(A): ¿Puedo empezar ahora?

SETH: Yes, you can start.

SETH: Sí, puedes empezar.

NARRATOR: Is everyone ready?

NARRADOR(A): ¿Todos están listos?

SARAH: Yes, we are all ready.

SARA: Sí, estamos todos listos.

NARRATOR: O.K. here we go. Once upon a time . . .

NARRADOR(A): Está bien, aquí vamos. Había una vez . . .

SALLY: Baa, baa

SALLY: Ba, ba

SARAH: Black sheep,

SARA: Una oveja negra,

SETH: Have you

SETH: ¿Tienes

SALLY: Any wool?

SALLY: Lana?

SARAH: Yes, sir

SARA: Sí, señor

SETH: Yes, sir

SETH: Sí, señor

From *Mother Goose Readers Theatre for Beginning Readers* by Anthony D. Fredericks. Westport, CT: Teacher Ideas Press. Copyright © 2007 by Anthony D. Fredericks.

SALLY: Three bags full:

SALLY: Tres bolsas llenas:

SARAH: One for the master,

SARA: Una para el dueño,

SETH: One for the dame,

SETH: Una para la dama,

SALLY: And one for . . .

SALLY: Y una para . . .

SARAH: The little boy

SARA: El pequeño niño

SETH: Who lives

SETH: Quien vive

ALL: Down the lane.

TODOS: Más abajo del camino.

NARRATOR: That was a good job.

NARRADOR(A): Eso fue un buen trabajo.

SALLY: Thank you. But I have a question.

SALLY: Gracias. Pero tengo una pregunta.

NARRATOR: What is it?

NARRADOR(A): ¿Qué es?

SALLY: What will the little boy do with the wool?

SALLY: ¿Qué hará el pequeño niño con la lana?

SARAH: He could make a shirt.

SARA: Él podría hacer una camisa.

SETH: He could make a sweater.

SETH: Él podría hacer un sueter.

NARRATOR: Or, he could make a jacket.

NARRADOR(A): O, él podría hacer una chaqueta.

SALLY: Oh, I see. Wool can be used for many things.

SALLY: Ah, yo entiendo. La lana puede ser usada para muchas cosas.

NARRATOR: You're right. Wool is very useful.

NARRADOR(A): Tienes razón. La lana es muy útil.

SARAH: So that's our story or the sheep and the wool.

SARA: Entonces ese es nuestro cuento de la oveja y la lana.

SETH: And, they all lived happily ever after.

SETH: Y, todos vivieron felices.

NARRATOR: That's right, happily ever after.

NARRADOR(A): Tiene razón, y fueron muy felices.

Pease Porridge Hot

PRESENTATION SUGGESTIONS

You may wish to explain to students that "pease porridge" is an old English term for thick pea soup. If students have never seen pea soup before, you may wish to bring in a can, open it, and pour it into a bowl for them to taste (please be aware of any food allergies).

PROPS

There should be some sort of table in the middle of the four Bears. If possible, place a pot or kettle in the middle of the table for added effect. Several wooden spoons could be placed inside the pot.

DELIVERY

The delivery should be light and fun. A little bit of silliness is also appropriate.

ORIGINAL VERSION

Pease porridge hot,
Pease porridge cold,
Pease porridge in the pot
Nine days old.
Some like it hot,
Some like it cold,
Some like it in the pot,
Nine days old.

COMPREHENSION ACTIVITY(IES)

1. Before sharing the rhyme with students, say the following to them:

    Close your eyes and create a picture in your head of a dinner table. In your picture, put a bright tablecloth on the table. Put a basket of flowers in the middle of the table. Put some bowls on the table. Put some spoons on the table. Place four chairs around the table. On one side of the table put a big pot. Look at the pot. There is steam coming from the top of the pot. Look at the steam coming from the top of the pot. There is something very hot inside the pot. Look down into the pot and see some soup. See some hot soup inside the pot. Look carefully at the soup. The soup is very thick. And, the soup is green. You are looking at thick green soup. Look at the thick green soup bubbling in the pot. You can almost smell the thick green soup bubbling in the pot. It smells so good. Now, slowly open your eyes and listen to this Mother Goose rhyme about thick soup.

2. Read the first four lines of this Mother Goose rhyme to students and then ask them some of the following predicting and inferring questions:

    "How did the porridge get hot?"
    "How did the porridge get cold?"
    "Why would someone let the porridge be nine days old?"

Pease Porridge Hot

STAGING: The characters should all be seated around a table—preferably a round table. They may be on stools or chairs. The narrator should be off to one side and seated on a tall stool.

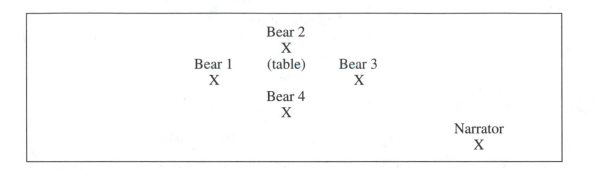

NARRATOR: This story opens inside the cabin of the Bear family.

BEAR 1: That's us.

BEAR 2: That's right. We're the Bears. The Big Bad Bears.

BEAR 3: Well, we aren't so big.

BEAR 4: And, we aren't so bad.

NARRATOR: They are really very nice bears. People just think that all bears are big and bad. But not these bears. This family of bears is really really nice.

BEAR 1: That's right, we're really really nice!

NARRATOR: O.K., now that the audience knows you are really nice, let's tell them a story.

BEAR 2: Yes, let's tell them a story.

BEAR 3: Yes, let's tell them a story about us.

BEAR 4: What a great idea!

NARRATOR: Hey, wait a minute. I'm the narrator. You guys are taking all my lines.

BEAR 1: We're sorry. We won't do it again!

BEAR 2: Yeah, we won't do it again.

BEAR 3: We promise.

BEAR 4: Yeah, we promise.

NARRATOR: [frustrated] O.K., O.K. Let's get started.

BEAR 1: We're all listening.

NARRATOR: Finally! Anyway, as I was saying, there was this family of bears. There was Papa Bear.

BEAR 1: That's me!

NARRATOR: There was Mama Bear.

BEAR 2: That's me!

NARRATOR: There was Big Brother Bear.

BEAR 3: That's me!

NARRATOR: And, there was Baby Sister Bear.

BEAR 4: That's me!

NARRATOR: One evening they all sat around the dinner table.

ALL BEARS: That's this [pointing to the table]!

NARRATOR: They were all hungry.

ALL BEARS: We were hungry.

NARRATOR: Well, Mama Bear made some thick pea soup for dinner. In the old days it wasn't called pea soup. It was called pease porridge.

BEAR 2: Yeah, some people thought it was cereal. But it wasn't.

BEAR 3: Some people thought it was yuck. But it wasn't.

BEAR 4: It was just really really thick soup.

NARRATOR: The soup was really thick. And it was cold. Really really cold.

BEAR 1: Yes, and it was something else.

NARRATOR: You're right. It was really really old.

BEAR 2: Yes, it had been sitting around for a long time.

BEAR 3: It was more than one week old.

BEAR 4: Yes, it was really about nine days old.

BEAR 3: EWWW! NINE DAYS OLD!!

NARRATOR: Anyway, the bears sat down to eat their nine day old soup. Then they had an idea.

BEAR 1: Yes, we had an idea.

BEAR 2: Hey, we said. Let's heat up the old soup. And, while it is heating we can sing a song.

BEAR 3: Yes, we can sing a song.

BEAR 4: Yes, the soup can heat and we can sing.

NARRATOR: And, so, the bears made up a song about their soup. They would now like to sing the song for you.

ALL BEARS: Yes, we would.

NARRATOR: So, here's the song about soup. Or the Bear's soup song. Or the soupy Bear's song about . . . .

ALL BEARS: LET'S GO!

NARRATOR: O.K., here they are.

BEAR 1: Pease porridge hot,

BEAR 2: Pease porridge cold,

BEAR 3: Pease porridge in the pot

BEAR 4: Nine days old.

BEAR 1: Some like it hot,

BEAR 2: Some like it cold,

BEAR 3: Some like it in the pot,

BEAR 4: Nine days old.

NARRATOR: And, that's the story about a pot of cold soup and four bears. The end.

From *Mother Goose Readers Theatre for Beginning Readers* by Anthony D. Fredericks. Westport, CT: Teacher Ideas Press. Copyright © 2007 by Anthony D. Fredericks.

To Market

PRESENTATION SUGGESTIONS

The presentation of this script should be informal. Each of the character's parts is relatively brief and friendly.

PROPS

If possible, you may wish to provide each of the girls in this play with a small basket. The baskets may be real or may be crafted out of construction paper. If possible, put an apron on each girl.

DELIVERY

Invite youngsters to talk in their conversational voices, much as they would if they were talking out on the playground.

ORIGINAL VERSION

To market, to market, to buy a fat pig,
Home again, home again, jiggety-jig.
To market, to market, to buy a fat hog,
Home again, home again, jiggety-jog.

COMPREHENSION ACTIVITY(IES)

1. Invite students to brainstorm all they know about shopping at a grocery store. As each suggestion is made, you may wish to record it on the chalkboard. Help students stay focused directly on grocery store shopping (items that can be purchased, what a grocery store looks like, etc.). After students have generated a list of about six to eight items, present them with some photographs of different types of grocery stores—from mega-stores to little country markets. Plan some time to discuss some of the similarities among these stores (they all use money; there are shelves) as well as some of the differences (some are very large, others small; some have neon signs, others hand-lettered signs).

2. Say the following to your students,

    Close your eyes. Now paint a picture of yourself. You are walking down a dirt path. In your hand you are holding a basket. The basket is red and white. There is nothing in the basket. The basket is empty. The sun overhead is bright. It is a sunny, warm summer day. You are walking down the path. Look ahead. There in the distance is a town. There are lots of buildings in the town. You look hard and see one building. It is a store. There are people going in and coming out of the store. Some have boxes full of groceries. Others have small bags with groceries. Still other people are loading their cars with lots and lots of groceries. Today, everybody is shopping at the store. They are all buying food. You get closer to the store. You are about to walk into the store. Then you see someone coming out of the store. The person you see has a big fat pig in her arms. Yes, she is carrying a big fat pig in her arms. "Why does she have a pig?" you ask yourself. But, there she is. She is walking out of the store with a big fat pig. A big, big fat pig. Now, slowly open your eyes and let's have some fun with a readers theatre story about three girls who went shopping for a big fat pig.

To Market

STAGING: The narrator should be off to the side of the staging area and may be seated or standing. The other characters should be standing in a loose semicircle.

		Girl 1	
Narrator	Boy	X	Girl 2
X	X		X
			Girl 3
			X

NARRATOR: Once upon a time there were three girls.

GIRL 1: There's me . . .

GIRL 2: . . . and me . . .

GIRL 3: . . . and me!

NARRATOR: One day they went to the store. On the way to the store they met a boy.

BOY: That's me!

NARRATOR: I guess I should let the characters [points to the players] tell you the rest of their story. O.K.?

BOY: Like the narrator was saying . . . . I was just walking along when these three girls came along. Hey, three girls, where are you going?

GIRL 1: We're going to the store.

BOY: What are you going to buy there?

GIRL 2: We want to but a pig.

BOY: Why do you want to buy a pig?

GIRL 3: Well, it's not just any pig. It's a fat pig!

BOY: O.K. Why do you want to buy a fat pig?

GIRL 1: Well, I guess we're very hungry.

BOY: Are the three of you going to eat one big fat pig?

GIRL 2: No, we might share the pig with our family.

BOY: Oh, so you must have a large family.

GIRL 3: Yes we do. We have lots of brothers and sisters and aunts and uncles and . . . .

BOY: O.K., you can stop there. I get the point.

GIRL 1: Anyway, there are a lot of people to feed at home. So we wanted to get something big.

GIRL 2: Something big that would feed all those people.

BOY: O.K., so you are going to the market to get a big fat pig. Then what?

GIRL 3: Well, then we're going to go home and fix the pig.

BOY: Is that all?

GIRL 1: Well, no. Because after we get the pig and take it home and fix it, then we have to go back to the market.

BOY: Why do you have to go back to the market again.

GIRL 2: Because then we have to get a hog.

BOY: You have to get a hog?

GIRL 3: That's right, a hog.

BOY: Let me guess. It's going to be a . . . a . . . a . . . fat hog! Right?

GIRL 1: That's right. After we get a fat pig, then we get a fat hog.

BOY: It seems like you like big fat animals.

GIRL 2: That's right. The fatter, the better.

BOY: So, let me get this straight. First you go to market.

GIRL 3: That's right.

BOY: And then you buy a fat pig?

GIRL 1: Right!

BOY: And then you take it home and fix it. Right?

GIRL 2: Right!

BOY: Then, you go back to the market?

GIRL 3: That's right!

BOY: And, now you buy a fat hog.

GIRL 1: You got it!

BOY: After you get this fat hog, you take it home, too.

GIRL 2: You're right!

BOY: And you fix the fat hog.

GIRL 3: That's the whole story.

BOY: Wow! It sounds like you girls have a very busy day.

GIRL 1: Yes, we do.

GIRL 2: But, there's one more thing we must do.

BOY: What's that?

GIRL 3: We must sing you the Mother Goose rhyme. O.K.?

BOY: O.K. I'm ready.

GIRL 1: To market,

GIRL 2: To market,

GIRL 3: To buy a fat pig,

GIRL 1: Home again,

GIRL 2: Home again,

GIRL 3: Jiggety-jig.

GIRL 1: To market,

GIRL 2: To market,

GIRL 3: To but a fat hog,

GIRL 1: Home again,

GIRL 2: Home again,

GIRL 3: Jiggety-jog.

NARRATOR: The end.

From *Mother Goose Readers Theatre for Beginning Readers* by Anthony D. Fredericks. Westport, CT: Teacher Ideas Press. Copyright © 2007 by Anthony D. Fredericks.

One for the Money

PRESENTATION SUGGESTIONS

This popular Mother Goose rhyme is short and sweet. You may wish to teach it to students ahead of time and at the appropriate place in the script invite the entire audience to say the rhyme along with the characters.

PROPS

No props are necessary for this script.

DELIVERY

All the characters should assume their "silly voices." Encourage students to play this script for laughs—make silly faces, use silly language, create silly movements.

ORIGINAL VERSION

One for the money,
And two for the show,
Three to get ready,
And four to go.

COMPREHENSION ACTIVITY(IES)

1. Invite students to talk about some of the predictions that they may make during the course of the day (e.g., what the weather will be like, what they will be having for dinner, etc.). Share with them the value of making predictions before listening to any story. Reflect on the predictions you may have made before reading the Mother Goose rhyme "One for the Money." For example: "When I heard the title I thought that this was going to be a story about someone finding lots and lots of money," or "When I saw the title I thought that this was a story about words that rhyme with 'money'." Invite students to talk about some other predictions that could be made for this rhyme.

One for the Money

STAGING: The characters may all be seated on tall stools or on chairs. The narrator may be placed behind a lectern or music stand.

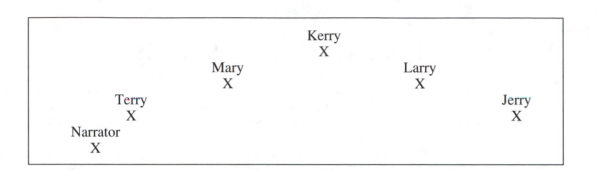

NARRATOR: Good morning. Today we have a short script for you. It's a silly story about numbers.

TERRY: I didn't know that numbers could be silly.

MARY: Well, I didn't know that either.

KERRY: I heard once that numbers could be silly.

LARRY: You know what? I think everybody here is silly! Who ever heard of silly numbers?

JERRY: I did.

TERRY: Well, guess what. Not only are numbers silly, but I think we are too.

MARY: What do you mean?

KERRY: I think she means that we all have silly names.

LARRY: Yeah, who gave us these names anyway.

JERRY: Just look at them [points to the signs around each player's neck].

TERRY: Hey, you're right. They are silly!

MARY: Yeah, they all rhyme.

KERRY: You're right. Look [points to each one]. There's Terry. There's Mary. There's Kerry . . . that's me!

LARRY: There's Larry . . . that's me. And, there's Jerry.

JERRY: Hey, let's say them all together.

TERRY: O.K., is everybody ready?

ALL: Yes.

TERRY: Then, let's go.

ALL: Terry, Mary, Kerry, Larry, Jerry!

MARY: That's cool. Let's do it again.

ALL: [faster] Terry, Mary, Kerry, Larry, Jerry!

KERRY: One more time!

ALL: [faster] Terry, Mary, Kerry, Larry, Jerry!

NARRATOR: Hey, can we get back to the story? It's really short. And, remember, just like your names, it's silly, too.

LARRY: O.K., I guess we can. What's the name of the story.

NARRATOR: The title of the story is "One for the Money."

JERRY: I wonder what that means.

NARRATOR: All I know is that it came from the country of England.

TERRY: O.K. So, are we ready to tell the story.

MARY: I think we are.

KERRY: So do I.

LARRY: Then, let's go.

JERRY: Yeah, let's go.

NARRATOR: And, now ladies and gentlemen, we present our silly short story called "One for the Money."

TERRY: One for the money,

From *Mother Goose Readers Theatre for Beginning Readers* by Anthony D. Fredericks. Westport, CT: Teacher Ideas Press. Copyright © 2007 by Anthony D. Fredericks.

MARY: And two for the show,

KERRY: Three to get ready,

LARRY: And four to go.

JERRY: Hey, you're right. That was a short story.

TERRY: Yup, that's all there is. There isn't any more.

MARY: Yes, we're all done.

KERRY: We're finished.

LARRY: The story is over.

JERRY: The end.

NARRATOR: [to audience] Thanks for listening. See you next time.

Little Boy Blue

PRESENTATION SUGGESTIONS

There is a touch of humor at the end of the script. You may wish to inform the players that some physical movement will be necessary at the end of the play (they will need to get off their chairs and lie down on the floor).

PROPS

You may wish to have a make-believe haystack for this script. This could be a pile of pillows on the floor or an illustration of a haystack projected on the wall with an overhead projector.

DELIVERY

The delivery should be lively and animated. You may wish to encourage students to do a little bit of over-acting for this script (to emphasize the humor).

ORIGINAL VERSION

Little Boy Blue,
Come blow your horn.
The sheep's in the meadow,
The cow's in the corn.
But where's the boy
Who looks after the sheep?
Under the haystack.
Fast asleep.
Will you wake him?
No, not I,
For if I do
He's sure to cry.

COMPREHENSION ACTIVITY(IES)

1. Tell students that you would like to have some of them retell the story. But before they retell what happened in the story, you are going to ask them a few questions. They should listen carefully to the questions and try to include answers to these questions in their retellings. Here are a few open-ended questions to get you started:

    — "What was the most interesting part of the story?"

    — "What did you enjoy most about this story?"

    — "What made you laugh?"

    — "Tell me how this story turned out."

    — "Is this story similar to other stories you have heard?"

    These open-ended queries are designed to help students focus on the essential elements that should be part of their retellings.

Little Boy Blue

Pequeño Niño Azul

STAGING: The characters may all be seated on stools. "Little Boy Blue" (who has a nonspeaking role) may be lying on the floor, pretending to be asleep.

Katy	Karl	Kathy	Kristen		Little Boy Blue
X	X	X	X		X
				Narrator	
				X	

NARRATOR: Welcome to our story.

NARRADOR(A): Bienvenidos a nuestro cuento.

KATY: It's a fun story.

KATY: Es un cuento divertido.

KARL: It's a story about a boy.

KARL: Es un cuento acerca de un niño.

KATHY: A boy all dressed in blue.

KATHY: Un niño vestido todo de azul.

KRISTEN: Why is he in blue?

KRISTEN: ¿Por qué está vestido de azul?

KATY: Maybe he likes blue.

KATY: Quizás le guste el azul.

KARL: I like blue.

KARL: A mi me gusta el azul.

From *Mother Goose Readers Theatre for Beginning Readers* by Anthony D. Fredericks. Westport, CT: Teacher Ideas Press. Copyright © 2007 by Anthony D. Fredericks.

KATHY: I like blue, too

KATHY: A mi me gusta el azul, también.

KRISTEN: Well, so do I.

KRISTEN: Bueno, a mi también.

KATY: I guess we all like blue.

KATY: Yo supongo que a todos nos gusta el azul.

NARRATOR: There's something else they [points to audience] need to know.

NARRADOR(A): Hay algo más que ellos [señalando a la audiencia] necesitan saber.

KARL: What's that?

KARL: ¿Qué?

NARRATOR: Well, our blue boy lives on a farm.

NARRADOR(A): Bueno, nuestro niño azul vive en una finca.

KATHY: How do you know that?

KATHY: ¿Cómo tú sabes eso?

NARRATOR: Well. I'm the narrator. I'm supposed to know everything.

NARRADOR(A): Bueno. Yo soy el narrador. Yo supuestamente debo saberlo todo.

KRISTEN: Oh, now I get it. You're the narrator because you know a lot of stuff.

KRISTEN: Ah, ahora yo entiendo. Tú eres el narrador porque sabes muchas cosas.

NARRATOR: Well, not really! I just know a lot of stuff about this story.

NARRADOR(A): ¡Bueno, realmente no! Yo sólo sé muchas cosas de este cuento.

KATY: Like the boy all dressed in blue.

KATY: Como el niño todo vestido de azul.

NARRATOR: Yes.

NARRADOR(A): Sí.

KARL: And the fact that he lives on a farm.

KARL: Y el hecho de que él vive en una finca.

NARRATOR: That's right.

NARRADOR(A): Así es.

KATHY: So, does that mean we can start the story?

KATHY: ¿Entonces, este significa que podemos empezar el cuento?

NARRATOR: I guess so. Is everybody ready?

NARRADOR(A): Yo supongo que sí. ¿Están listos todos?

KRISTEN: I think we are.

KRISTEN: Pienso que estamos listos.

NARRATOR: All right. Ladies and gentlemen, we now present the story about a little boy. He was all dressed in blue. And he lived on a farm. Let's go!

NARRADOR(A): Muy bien. Damas y Caballeros, ahora le presentamos el cuento acerca del niño. Todo vestido de azul. Y él vivía en una finca. ¡Vamos!

KATY: Little boy blue,

KATY: Pequeño niño azul,

KARL: Come, blow your horn.

KARL: Ven, toca tu trompeta.

KATHY: The sheep's in the meadow,

KATHY: Las ovejas en el prado,

KRISTEN: The cow's in the corn.

KRISTEN: La vaca en el campo de maíz.

KATY: Where's the little boy

KATY: ¿Dónde está el pequeño niño . . .

KARL: Who looks after the sheep?

KARL: . . . el cual cuida la oveja?

KATHY: [points to Little Boy Blue] He's under the haystack

KATHY: [señalando a Pequeño Niño Azul] Él está debajo del heno

KRISTEN: Fast asleep.

KRISTEN: Durmiendo.

NARRATOR: That was a good story. You did a good job.

NARRADOR(A): Ese fue un cuento bueno. Ustedes hicieron un buen trabajo.

KATY: I'm tired from that story.

KATY: Estoy cansada con ese cuento.

KARL: So am I.

KARL: Yo también.

KATHY: I'm tired, too.

KATY: Yo estoy cansada, también.

KRISTEN: And so am I.

KRISTEN: Y yo también.

[The four main characters get off their stools or chairs and go over to Little Boy Blue. They all lie down on the floor and pretend to go to sleep. They may begin snoring quietly.]

[Los cuatro personajes principales dejan las sillas y van al Pequeño Niño Azul. Ellos se acuestan en el suelo y finjen estar dormidos. Ellos pueden empezar a roncar con suavemente.]

NARRATOR: Well, our story's done. Everybody worked hard. Now they are all tired. Good night everyone.

NARRADOR(A): Bueno, nuestro cuento se acabó. Todos trabajaron duro. Ahora todos están cansados. Buenas noches a todos.

Sing a Song of Sixpence

PRESENTATION SUGGESTIONS

You may wish to explain to students that in merry old England it was perfectly acceptable to eat songbirds (in fact, it still is in parts of Italy). Pies today are considered desserts, but in the "old days" all sorts of meats and other food items were put into pastry shells and served as the main course.

PROPS

You may wish to place a fake pie on a small table in the middle of the staging area.

DELIVERY

The king should be boastful and demanding. The servant should be condescending. The three black-birds should be perky and happy.

ORIGINAL VERSION

Sing a song of sixpence,
A pocket full of rye;
Four and twenty blackbirds
Baked in a pie!
When the pie was opened,
The birds began to sing!
Wasn't that a dainty dish
To set before the king.

The king was in his counting house,
Counting out his money.
The Queen was in the parlour,
Eating bread and honey.
The maid was in the garden,
Hanging out the clothes
When along came a blackbird,
And snipped off her nose!

(NOTE: Most collections of Mother Goose rhymes delete the second stanza. The maid hanging out the wash is a reference to Anne Boleyn, one of the wives of Henry VIII who, as you will recall, lost her head [" . . . snipped off her nose!"]. The "blackbird" refers to her executioner.)

COMPREHENSION ACTIVITY(IES)

1. Invite a selected student to retell the rhyme (first stanza only). Ask other students to listen carefully. When the retelling is complete, prompt the students with some of the following questions:

    – "What did he or she include in the retelling?"

    – "What did he or she include in the introduction?"

    – "What else could we add to the retelling?"

    – "What happens next?"

    – "What should we include in the end of the retelling?"

    – "What do you think might happen next?"

2. Invite students to participate in a discussion about all the different kinds of pies that they know about. Ask students to brainstorm for all the various pies they can remember eating or seeing in a restaurant or grocery store. They may also wish to talk with their parents about various types of pies. Make a running list on the chalkboard of the various pies they suggest. You may wish to provide students with some old magazines (e.g., *Good Housekeeping,* etc.) that have pie recipes. Invite students to cut out pictures of various pies and create a "Pie Collage" to be posted on a bulletin board. You may wish to challenge students to obtain at least 20 different pies for their display. Plan some time to talk about the wide variety of pies (dessert and main course) that are eaten in this country as well as around the world.

Sing a Song of Sixpence

STAGING: The characters may all be seated on tall stools or on chairs. The narrator should be off to the side and may be seated at a lectern or in front of a music stand.

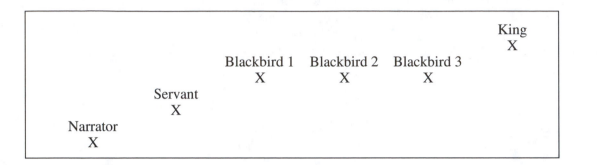

NARRATOR: Once upon a time there was a king. He was a very hungry king. He always liked to eat. His servants were always bringing him food. But, one day there wasn't enough food in the castle. That is how our story begins.

KING: Hey, I'm hungry. Bring me some food!

SERVANT: I'm sorry, Mr. King, there is not food!

KING: What do you mean?

SERVANT: There is no food in the castle.

KING: I can't believe that! Why is there no food in the castle?

SERVANT: Well, Mr. King, somebody forgot to go to the store and get some food this week.

KING: I want that person fired.

SERVANT: It was me, sir.

KING: Oh, well in that case, you can stay. You are a good servant.

SERVANT: Thank you, Mr. King.

KING: But, I'm still hungry. What will I do?

SERVANT: I can go and ask the cook. Maybe he knows what to do.

KING: O.K. I'll wait until you get back.

NARRATOR: So, the servant went to talk to the cook. The cook thought and thought. Then he had a brilliant idea. He would bake the king a pie. It wouldn't be just any pie. It would be a special pie. It would be a pie filled with birds. That's right—a pie filled with birds. Let's watch and see.

SERVANT: Hey, Mr. King, I've come back from the kitchen. The cook has made something special for you. It's a pie.

KING: Yum, yum. I love to eat pie.

SERVANT: I think you'll like this one. It's a bird pie.

KING: A BIRD PIE!!!

BLACKBIRD 1: Yes, we are all in the pie.

BLACKBIRD 2: Yes, the pie is jammed packed with lots and lots of birds.

BLACKBIRD 3: Yes, there are 24 blackbirds jammed into this delicious pie.

KING: Why would I want to eat 24 blackbirds? What do they taste like?

BLACKBIRD 1: We taste good.

BLACKBIRD 2: Yes, we are the best tasting birds in the world.

BLACKBIRD 3: You bet! We are really delicious.

KING: I don't know. I've never eaten blackbirds before. What do they taste like.

BLACKBIRD 1: Some people say we taste like chicken.

BLACKBIRD 2: Some people say we taste like roast beef.

From *Mother Goose Readers Theatre for Beginning Readers* by Anthony D. Fredericks. Westport, CT: Teacher Ideas Press. Copyright © 2007 by Anthony D. Fredericks.

BLACKBIRD 3: And, some people say we taste like . . . well, like . . . like blackbird.

KING: I'm not so sure.

SERVANT: I think you'll really enjoy this pie. It's not a cherry pie. Or, an apple pie. Or, even a chocolate pie. It's a blackbird pie.

BLACKBIRD 1: Yum, Yum!

BLACKBIRD 2: Yum, Yum!

BLACKBIRD 3: Yes, Yum, Yum!

NARRATOR: And, so it was. The hungry king decided to eat the blackbird pie. He ate all 24 of the blackbirds in the pie. He said that he liked it. Do you think you [points to audience] would like to eat some blackbird pie?

AUDIENCE: NO!!!

NARRATOR: I didn't think so. But, I think you would like to hear the rhyme that was written for this story. Here goes.

BLACKBIRD 1: Sing a song of sixpence,

BLACKBIRD 2: A pocket full of rye;

BLACKBIRD 3: Four and twenty blackbirds

KING: Baked in a pie!

BLACKBIRD 1: When the pie was opened,

BLACKBIRD 2: The birds began to sing!

BLACKBIRD 3: Wasn't that a dainty dish

KING: To set before the king?

Here We Go Round the Mulberry Bush

PRESENTATION SUGGESTIONS

This script is light and fun. The characters make fun of their abilities (talking) in addition to making fun of the author (me). A little practice before the actual presentation will help characters become comfortable with their lines and keep the emphasis on fun.

PROPS

Place some sort of potted plant in the middle of the staging area. A bush is preferred, but is not absolutely necessary.

DELIVERY

The characters should have a somewhat perplexed expression on their faces as they deliver their lines. They should be questioning their parts as well as the motives of the writer. They are, after all, talking animals.

ORIGINAL VERSION

Here we go round the mulberry bush,
The mulberry bush, the mulberry bush,
Here we go round the mulberry bush,
On a cold and frosty morning.

This is the way we wash our hands,
Wash our hands, wash our hands,
This is the way we wash our hands,
On a cold and frosty morning.

This is the way we wash our clothes,
Wash our clothes, wash our clothes,
This is the way we wash our clothes,
On a cold and frosty morning.

(NOTE: Most collections of Mother Goose rhymes eliminate the last two stanzas. However, over the years this rhyme has lent itself to many different additions of everyday activities. It is an ideal rhyme for students to contribute their own ideas about familiar tasks. ["This is the way we skip our rope," "This is the way we clean and sweep."])

COMPREHENSION ACTIVITY(IES)

1.   Invite students, in small groups, to draw an illustration to accompany the rhyme. Be sure to encourage them to use some of the details from the rhyme in their illustrations. Plan some time to discuss the illustrations and the specific details that were included. Help children see the connections between the details of the rhyme and the details in their illustrations.

2.   As an extension of the activity above, invite students to create their own verses for this rhyme (see the Note above). Invite the class to select four brand new verses. Divide the class into four groups. After singing the additional verses of the rhyme, invite each group to work together to design an illustration of a selected verse that displays the important details. Plan time for each group to describe its illustration.

Here We Go Round the Mulberry Bush

STAGING: The characters should be standing during this script. They may choose to move around the staging area as they are speaking or may wish to stand in a loose semi-circle around a potted bush. The narrator should stand off to the side and in back of the players.

```
                                                          Narrator
                                                             X
                Dog 2                    Cat 1
                  X                        X
   Dog 1                                          Cat 2
     X                    (bush)                    X
```

NARRATOR: Once upon a time, in England, there were lots of mulberry bushes. A mulberry bush is both green and red. It's a very pretty bush. Sometimes people would dry their clothes on these bushes. Then, their clothes would have a very nice smell. Today, there aren't many mulberry bushes in England. But people still like them. So do animals.

DOG 1: Hey, look. It's a mulberry bush [points].

DOG 2: Hey, you're right. I haven't seen one of those in a long time.

CAT 1: I haven't either.

CAT 2: It sure smells nice.

DOG 1: Yes, it does. It has a pretty smell.

DOG 2: I wonder what why it's here.

CAT 1: Maybe the writer did that.

CAT 2: Why would he do that?

DOG 1: Writers are strange like that.

DOG 2: They sure are!

CAT 1: Yes, I think the writer is very strange. He put all of us around a mulberry bush.

CAT 2: Then he did something that was really strange.

DOG 1: What's that?

CAT 2: He made all of us talk.

DOG 2: Hey, you're right. We're talking animals!

CAT 1: Yes, we are. Now, you know [points to audience] that animals can't talk.

DOG 1: Right. Some of us just bark and woof all day long.

CAT 2: And some of us just meow and purr all day long.

DOG 2: So this must be a really strange author. Because he gave us words to say.

CAT 1: And, we really can't say words.

DOG 1: But, this is make-believe.

CAT 2: And, this is a make-believe story.

DOG 2: And the writer is really really strange. So guess what?

CAT 1: That's right. We're talking animals.

DOG 1: Yeah, we're talking animals standing around a mulberry bush.

CAT 2: So, what do we do now?

DOG 2: I guess we should ask the narrator. The narrator always knows everything.

CAT 1: Hey, narrator person. What do we do next?

NARRATOR: Well, it says here [points to script] that you four characters should dance around the mulberry bush and sing a song.

DOG 1: Dance around a mulberry bush. Why would we do that?

CAT 2: Maybe the writer of this story thinks that we are as crazy as he is.

DOG 2: That must be very crazy! What else do we have to do?

CAT 1: We have to sing.

DOG 1: Boy, that is very strange. First we talk. Then, we have to dance.

CAT 2: . . . and then, we have to sing a song.

DOG 2: This is the strangest story I've ever been in.

CAT 1: Me too. But, I'm getting hungry, so what do you say we do our story, and then we can go and get some lunch?

DOG 1: Sounds good to me.

CAT 2: Me, too.

DOG 2: And, me too.

NARRATOR: So the four animals stood around the mulberry bush. They all held hands and began to dance around the bush. And, they began to sing.

[The characters hold hands and move around the potted bush while they say their lines.]

DOG 1: Here we go round the mulberry bush,

DOG 2: The mulberry bush, the mulberry bush,

CAT 1: Here we go round the mulberry bush,

CAT 2: On a cold and frosty morning.

NARRATOR: One more time.

[The characters again hold hands and move around the potted bush while they say their lines.]

DOG 1: Here we go round the mulberry bush,

DOG 2: The mulberry bush, the mulberry bush,

CAT 1: Here we go round the mulberry bush,

CAT 2: On a cold and frosty morning.

DOG 1: Yes, you're right. The writer sure is a strange person!

Old King Cole

PRESENTATION SUGGESTIONS

Your may wish to read this rhyme to students before they produce it as a readers theatre production. Mention to them that the information about the pipe, bowl, and fiddlers three is true. The pipe was probably some kind of wind instrument popular in the Middle Ages. The bowl was most likely an instrument similar to the Irish bodhran drum.

PROPS

You may wish to provide the fiddlers with make-believe fiddles (one stick for a bow and another stick for a fiddle). Provide the king with a bowl and a make-believe pipe (another stick).

DELIVERY

The king should be happy and proud. The fiddlers should be happy and merry. The narrator should appear knowledgeable and learned.

ORIGINAL VERSION

Old King Cole
Was a merry old soul,
And a merry old soul was he.
He called for his pipe,
And he called for his bowl,
And he called for his fiddlers three.

Every fiddler he had a fiddle,
And a very fine fiddle had he.
Oh there's none so rare,
As can compare,
With King Cole and his fiddlers three.

COMPREHENSION ACTIVITY(IES)

1. Invite students to provide a retelling of the story (first stanza). You may wish to use some of the following prompts:

    – "What should we include in a retelling of this story?"

    – "What should we include in an introduction?"

    – "Can you be a little more specific?"

    – "How can we continue retelling?"

    – "What happened next?"

    – "If we could keep going, what would happen next in the story?"

2. As appropriate, you may wish to engage youngsters in a variation of the game show *Jeopardy!*®. Initially, you can demonstrate this by providing an "answer" for youngsters (e.g., "bowl") and then providing an appropriate question for that "answer" ("What was the second thing Old King Cole asked for?"). Repeat this several times. As children become more practiced, invite them to offer questions for some "answers" that you provide. In this activity, children learn the art of question asking by watching you as you model appropriate answers as well as appropriate questions.

Old King Cole

El Viejo Rey Col

STAGING: The narrator is seated on a tall stool. The speaking characters (Jack and Jill) may also be seated on tall stools. The nonspeaking characters (three fiddlers) should be standing. King Cole should be seated on a chair.

```
King Cole                          Three Fiddlers
   X                                  X  X  X

              Jack        Jill
               X           X

                                        Narrator
                                           X
```

NARRATOR: This is an interesting story from long ago.

NARRADOR(A): Este es un cuento interesante de hace mucho tiempo.

JACK: How long ago did this story happen?

JUAN: ¿Cuánto hace que pasó este cuento?

NARRATOR: It happened many years ago in England.

NARRADOR(A): Pasó hace muchos años en Inglaterra.

JILL: I know where England is. It's a country on the other side of the Atlantic Ocean.

JUANA: Yo sé donde está Inglaterra. Es un país en el otro lado del océano Atlántico.

NARRATOR: You're right. Anyway, this is a story about a king who lived many years ago.

NARRADOR(A): Tienes razón. En todo caso, esto es un cuento sobre un rey quien vivió hace mucho tiempo.

JACK: What was his name again, I forgot?

JUAN: ¿Cómo se llamaba, otra vez, se me olvidó?

NARRATOR: His name was Cole. Everybody called him Old King Cole.

NARRADOR(A): Su nombre era Col. Todo el mundo le llamaba el Viejo Rey Col.

JILL: Did everybody like him?

JUANA: ¿Le caía bien él a todo el mundo?

NARRATOR: I think so. If they didn't like him, they wouldn't have made up this story about him.

NARRADOR(A): Pienso que sí. Si no le hubiese caido bien, ellos no hubiesen hecho un cuento sobre él.

JACK: I guess you're right. What else should we know about King Cole?

JUAN: Yo supongo que tienes razón. ¿Qué más debemos saber sobre el Rey Col?

NARRATOR: He really liked his music.

NARRADOR(A): A él le gustaba la música.

JILL: How do you know that?

JUANA: ¿Cómo sabes eso?

NARRATOR: Well, why don't the two of you [points to Jack and Jill] tell the story? When you're done, I'll tell you some more about this old king.

NARRADOR(A): Bueno, ¿por qué no ustedes dos [señalando a Juan y Juana] cuentan el cuento? Cuando terminen, les diré un poco más sobre este viejo rey.

From *Mother Goose Readers Theatre for Beginning Readers* by Anthony D. Fredericks. Westport, CT: Teacher Ideas Press. Copyright © 2007 by Anthony D. Fredericks.

JACK: O.K., I'm ready. What about you, Jill?

JUAN: Está bien, estoy listo. ¿Qué tal tú, Juana?

JILL: I'm ready. Let's go.

JUANA: Estoy lista. Vamos.

JACK: Old King Cole [points to King Cole]

JUAN: El Viejo Rey Col [señalando al Rey Col]

[King Cole smiles and waves to the audience.]

[El Rey Col sonrie y saluda a la audiencia.]

JILL: Was a merry old soul,

JUANA: Era un alma vieja y alegre,

[King Cole laughs out loud.]

[El Rey Col se rie en voz alta.]

JACK: And a merry old soul was he;

JUAN: Y un alma vieja y alegre;

[King Cole laughs again.]

[El Rey Col se rie otra vez.]

JILL: He called for his pipe,

JUANA: Él llamó por su pipa,

[King Cole waves to someone off stage.]

[El Rey Col saluda a alguien fuera de la tarima.]

JACK: And he called for his bowl,

JUAN: Y él llamó por su vasija,

[King Cole waves to someone else off stage.]

[El Rey Col saluda a alguien más fuera de la tarima.]

JILL: And he called for his fiddlers three.

JUANA: Y él llamó a sus tres violinistas.

KING COLE: Hey, fiddlers, come here and play.

REY COL: Oigan, violinistas, vengan aquí y toquen.

[The fiddlers come over to the King and pretend to play fiddles.]

[Los violinistas vienen donde el Rey y fingen tocar los violines.]

NARRATOR: So, what do you think?

NARRADOR(A): ¿Entonces, qué piensan?

JACK: I like the way it rhymes.

JUAN: Me gusta la manera en que rima.

JILL: Me, too.

JUANA: A mi, también.

NARRATOR: Well let me tell you something else.

NARRADOR(A): Bueno, permítanme decirles algo más.

JACK: What's that?

JUAN: ¿Qué?

NARRATOR: Well, since this is an old story there are words that don't mean the same thing as the words we use today.

NARRADOR(A): Bueno, porque este es un cuento viejo hay palabras que no tienen el mismo sentido como las palabras que usamos hoy en día.

JILL: What do you mean?

JUANA: ¿Qué quieres decir con eso?

NARRATOR: Well, the pipe is some kind of musical instrument. It's not something he used to smoke.

NARRADOR(A): Bueno, la pipa es una clase de instrumento. No es algo que se usa para fumar.

JACK: That's interesting. So, the old king played a musical instrument.

JUAN: Eso es interesante. Entonces, el viejo rey tocaba un instrumento musical.

NARRATOR: That's right. And, something else.

NARRADOR(A): Así es. Y, algo más.

JILL: What's that?

JUANA: ¿Qué?

NARRATOR: The bowl was probably a drum, not something to put food in.

NARRADOR(A): La vasija era probablemente un tambor, no algo para poner comida.

JACK: So the old king played a pipe instrument . . .

JUAN: Entonces, el viejo rey tocaba un instrumento . . .

From *Mother Goose Readers Theatre for Beginning Readers* by Anthony D. Fredericks. Westport, CT: Teacher Ideas Press. Copyright © 2007 by Anthony D. Fredericks.

JILL: . . . and a drum . . .

JUANA: . . . y un tambor . . .

NARRATOR: . . . and he had three fiddlers to play music for him, too.

NARRADOR(A): . . . y él tenía tres violinistas para tocar música para él, también.

JACK: So, there was a lot of music in the old days in England.

JUAN: Entonces, había mucha música en el pasado en Inglaterra.

JILL: Yes, I guess there was.

JUANA: Sí, supongo que la había.

NARRATOR: Maybe that's why he was a "merry old soul."

NARRADOR(A): Quizás por eso él era un "alma vieja y alegre."

Little Bo-Peep

PRESENTATION SUGGESTIONS

The presentation should be light and airy. There is no heavy message in this script and the characters can all play their parts for fun.

PROPS

No props are necessary for this script.

DELIVERY

Bo-Peep can be somewhat confused and unknowing. The four narrators should be concerned and inquisitive.

ORIGINAL VERSION

Little Bo-Peep has lost her sheep,
And can't tell where to find them.
Leave them alone,
And they'll come home,
Wagging their tails behind them.

COMPREHENSION ACTIVITY(IES)

1. Model for the students some of the types of questions you might ask yourself as you read this rhyme. Focus on those questions that establish a "connection" between prior experiences and the experiences of Bo-Peep in the story. For example, you might ask (out loud) these questions:

    – "I wonder if Bo-Peep always loses things like I do sometimes?"

    – "Will she look in a hundred different places like I do when I lose my car keys?"

    – "Will she worry about the sheep like I sometimes worry about my children?"

Little Bo-Peep

STAGING: This script has four narrators and a single character (Bo-Peep). Bo-Peep should be seated on a tall stool or a chair. The narrators can be walking around the staging area or can be formed into a loose semicircle.

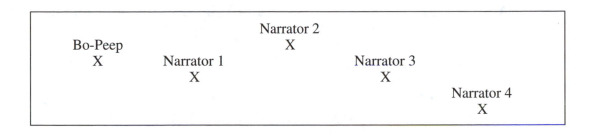

NARRATOR 1: Once there was this little girl.

NARRATOR 2: There she is over there [points to Bo-Peep].

NARRATOR 1: Now, this little girl was always losing things.

BO-PEEP: Yes, I always lose things. I would lose my head if it wasn't on tight.

NARRATOR 3: That's true.

BO-PEEP: I sometimes lose my car keys.

NARRATOR 4: Hey, wait a minute. You're Little Bo-Peep. You don't have a car!

BO-PEEP: You're right. I almost forget!

NARRATOR 1: Anyway, this little girl always forgot things.

NARRATOR 2: One day she lost her hat.

NARRATOR 3: Another day she lost her shoes.

NARRATOR 4: And, one day she lost her library book and had to pay a fine.

BO-PEEP: That's right. I lose a lot of things. And, sometimes, I have to pay for them.

From *Mother Goose Readers Theatre for Beginning Readers* by Anthony D. Fredericks. Westport, CT: Teacher Ideas Press. Copyright © 2007 by Anthony D. Fredericks.

NARRATOR 1: Any way, as I was saying. This little girl always lost stuff.

NARRATOR 2: Yes, she always lost stuff.

NARRATOR 3: Well, one day, she lost her sheep. I mean, can you [points to audience] believe that. SHE LOST HER SHEEP!!!

NARRATOR 4: Hey, wait a minute. Why did this little girl [points to Bo-Peep] have sheep in the first place?

NARRATOR 1: I don't know. Do you know [looks at Narrator 2]?

NARRATOR 2: I don't know either [turns to Narrator 3]. Do you know why this little girl [points to Bo-Peep] had some sheep?

NARRATOR 3: I sure don't know. Let's ask her. Hey, Bo-Peep girl, why did you have some sheep in the first place?

BO-PEEP: I can't remember. I think I was taking care of them for my farmer friend.

NARRATOR 4: Well, O.K. But how did you lose them?

BO-PEEP: I just don't know. One day I was just minding my business walking down the road with my sheep. The next thing I know the police were asking me some questions about the missing sheep.

NARRATOR 1: Where did the police come from?

BO-PEEP: I don't know. They just show up in these mysteries all the time.

NARRATOR 2: Then, what happened?

BO-PEEP: Well, the police asked me lots of questions. They wanted to know how someone could lose about 347 sheep in the middle of the day.

NARRATOR 3: So, what did you tell them?

BO-PEEP: I told them the truth. I said, "I didn't know. I said that I was walking down the road with my 347 sheep and the next thing I knew the sheep were all gone. Just like that, they disappeared."

NARRATOR 4: Well, maybe they'll come back all on their own.

BO-PEEP: Do you really think so?

NARRATOR 1: That's what always happens in these Mother Goose stories.

BO-PEEP: Gosh, I didn't know that. Hmmmmm.

NARRATOR 2: But, there's one more mystery still left to solve.

BO-PEEP: What's that?

NARRATOR 2: How did you get that funny name? I've never heard anyone called Bo-Peep before. That's a weird name.

BO-PEEP: Yes, it is. I think that Old Mother Goose gave me the name.

NARRATOR 3: She sure is a strange duck.

NARRATOR 4: Or, goose!

BO-PEEP: So, how would you all [points to the 4 narrators] like to do the rhyme? O.K.

NARRATOR 1: O.K., here we go! Little Bo-Peep . . .

NARRATOR 2: . . . has lost her sheep,

NARRATOR 3: And can't tell . . .

NARRATOR 4: . . . where to find them.

NARRATOR 1: Leave them alone,

NARRATOR 2: And they'll come home,

NARRATOR 3: Wagging their tails . . .

NARRATOR 4: . . . behind them.

From *Mother Goose Readers Theatre for Beginning Readers* by Anthony D. Fredericks. Westport, CT: Teacher Ideas Press. Copyright © 2007 by Anthony D. Fredericks.

Peter Pumpkin-Eater

PRESENTATION SUGGESTIONS

Inform students in advance that this script will give them an opportunity to practice their speed of reading. After one group of four students presents their version, invite another group of four to try their hand at this script.

PROPS

No props are necessary.

DELIVERY

The emphasis in this script is on speed. The first reading should be at a normal rate; the second reading a little faster; the third reading even faster; and the fourth reading the fastest of all. Let students know that making mistakes is O.K.—the emphasis is on the fun that can be had with a rapid delivery.

ORIGINAL VERSION

Peter, Peter, pumpkin-eater,
Had a wife and couldn't keep her.
He put her in a pumpkin shell,
And there he kept her very well.

COMPREHENSION ACTIVITY(IES)

1. As part of a follow-up discussion about this Mother Goose rhyme, you may wish to ask students some selected "What if" questions. Here are a few to get you started:

    – "What if Peter had to live inside the pumpkin?"

    – "What if Peter's whole family had to live inside the pumpkin?"

    – "What if your family had to live inside a pumpkin?"

    – "What if Peter's wife had to live inside a lemon?"

    – "What if Peter's wife had to live inside a watermelon?"

Peter Pumpkin-Eater

STAGING: There is no narrator for this story. The four characters do not have names, only numbers. They should be standing around in either a loose circle or a straight line facing the audience.

```
                        Number 2
                           X
        Number 1                        Number 3
           X                               X
                   Number 4
                      X
```

NUMBER 1: Peter, Peter

NUMBER 2: Pumpkin-eater,

NUMBER 3: Had a wife . . .

NUMBER 4: . . . and couldn't keep her.

NUMBER 1: He put her in . . .

NUMBER 2: . . . a pumpkin shell,

NUMBER 3: And there he kept her . . .

NUMBER 4: . . . very well.

[faster]

NUMBER 1: Peter, Peter

NUMBER 2: Pumpkin-eater,

NUMBER 3: Had a wife . . .

NUMBER 4: . . . and couldn't keep her.

NUMBER 1: He put her in . . .

NUMBER 2: . . . a pumpkin shell,

NUMBER 3: And there he kept her . . .

NUMBER 4: . . . very well.

[faster]

NUMBER 1: Peter, Peter

NUMBER 2: Pumpkin-eater,

NUMBER 3: Had a wife . . .

NUMBER 4: . . . and couldn't keep her.

NUMBER 1: He put her in . . .

NUMBER 2: . . . a pumpkin shell,

NUMBER 3: And there he kept her . . .

NUMBER 4: . . . very well.

[faster]

NUMBER 1: Peter, Peter

NUMBER 2: Pumpkin-eater,

NUMBER 3: Had a wife . . .

NUMBER 4: . . . and couldn't keep her.

NUMBER 1: He put her in . . .

NUMBER 2: . . . a pumpkin shell,

NUMBER 3: And there he kept her . . .

NUMBER 4: . . . very well.

ALL: The end.

Mary Had a Little Lamb

PRESENTATION SUGGESTIONS

You may wish to discuss the meaning of the word "fleece" (a coat of wool, as on a sheep) before starting this script. You may wish to play some pastoral music in the background for added effect.

PROPS

If possible, provide the Detective with an overcoat or some type of special costume. You may wish to project an illustration of Mary and the lamb on a wall in back of the players.

DELIVERY

The Detective should be self-assured and bold. The two narrators should have perplexed expressions on their faces—this will add to the humor.

ORIGINAL VERSION

Mary had a little lamb,
Its fleece was white as snow.
And everywhere that Mary went,
The lamb was sure to go

It followed her to school one day,
Which was against the rule.
It made the children laugh and play
To see a lamb at school.

COMPREHENSION ACTIVITY(IES)

1.   Before reading this rhyme or performing the script, you may wish to use the following imagery activity:

I want everybody to close their eyes. Now, I want you to paint a picture in your head. Make a farm. It's a big farm. There is a house. There is a barn. There is a garden. There is a field. Look carefully and you will see some animals on the farm. You will see some cows. The cows are munching grass. Look again and you will see some sheep. The sheep are in a field. They are also munching some grass. There are big sheep and there are small sheep. The small sheep are called lambs. They are walking around. The lambs are eating and making noises. The lambs are looking for their mothers. Oh, look. Over there is a little girl. She is dressed in a blue dress. She is walking over to the sheep. She sees one of the lambs. She walks up to the lamb. She reaches out and pets the lamb. The lamb makes a sound. The girl pets the lamb again. The girl starts to walk away. The little lamb starts to follow the girl. The girl walks. The lamb follows her. The girl goes to the house. The lamb goes to the house. The lamb is following the girl. Wherever the girl goes, the lamb goes, too. Now, I want you to slowly open your eyes. Think about the picture you made in your head. Think about that picture as I share this rhyme [or as we share this readers theatre script]. The name of the rhyme [script] is "Mary Had a Little Lamb."

Mary Had a Little Lamb

María Tenía un Pequeño Cordero

STAGING: The characters should all be standing. They may be placed at individual lecterns or may hold the scripts in their hands.

Narrator 1	Detective	Narrator 2
X	X	X

NARRATOR 1: Ladies and gentlemen. We have a mystery. Because we have a mystery, we've called a world famous detective.

NARRADOR(A) 1: Damas y Caballeros. Tenemos un misterio. Y porque tenemos un misterio, llamamos un famoso detective del mundo.

DETECTIVE: That's me!

DETECTIVE: ¡Ese soy yo!

NARRATOR 1: Yes, that's [points to Detective] the world famous detective. He (she) can solve any case. Even a case of a little lamb.

NARRADOR(A) 1: Sí, ese es [señalando al Detective] el famoso detective del mundo. Él (ella) puede resolver cualquier caso. Inclusive el caso sobre el pequeño cordero.

DETECTIVE: Wait a minute! You told me this was a big robbery . . . not a story about a cute little lamb.

DETECTIVE: ¡Espérate un minuto! Tú me dijiste que esto fue un robo grande . . . no un cuento sobre un lindo pequeño cordero!

From *Mother Goose Readers Theatre for Beginning Readers* by Anthony D. Fredericks. Westport, CT: Teacher Ideas Press. Copyright © 2007 by Anthony D. Fredericks.

NARRATOR 1: Well, we didn't tell you everything. But we really need your help.

NARRADOR(A) 1: Bueno, nosotros no te dijimos todo. Pero nosotros necesitamos realmente tu ayuda.

DETECTIVE: Well, I guess I can help you. I'm not doing anything right now.

DETECTIVE: Bueno, yo supongo que puedo ayudarte. Yo no estoy haciendo nada ahora mismo.

NARRATOR 1: That's good. Now here's the deal. My friend over there [points to Narrator 2] will tell the story.

NARRADOR(A) 1: Está bien. Ahora este es el trato. Mi amigo allá [señalando al Narrador 2] va a contra el cuento.

DETECTIVE: Let me see if I have this right. Your friend over there [points to Narrator 2] . . . .

DETECTIVE: Déjame ver si entiendo todo. Tu amigo allá [señalando al Narrador 2] . . . .

NARRATOR 1: Yes, my friend over there [points to Narrator 2] . . . .

NARRADOR(A) 1: Sí, mi amigo allá [señalando al Narrador 2] . . . .

DETECTIVE: HMMM, I think I have solved the case.

DETECTIVE: HMMM, yo pienso que he resuelto el caso.

NARRATOR 1: Wait a minute. I haven't even finished my part.

NARRADOR(A) 1: Esperate un minuto. Ni siquiera he terminado mi parte.

DETECTIVE: Oh, I'm sorry.

DETECTIVE: Oh, lo siento.

NARRATOR 1: O.K., my friend over there [points] will tell you the story. You can ask questions. We'll answer the questions. Then, you can solve the case.

NARRADOR(A) 1: Está bien, mi amigo allá [señalando] va a contarte el cuento. Tú puedes hacer preguntas. Nosotros contestarémos las preguntas. Luego, tú puedes resolver el caso.

DETECTIVE: I'm pretty smart, so this shouldn't take long.

DETECTIVE: Soy bastante listo, entonces esto no debe tomar mucho tiempo.

NARRATOR 1: Are you ready [points], world famous detective?

NARRADOR(A) 1: ¿Estás listo [señalando], famoso detective del mundo?

DETECTIVE: I'm ready.

DETECTIVE: Estoy listo.

NARRATOR 1: Are you ready [points], Narrator 2?

NARRADOR(A) 1: ¿Estás listo [señalando], Narrador 2?

NARRATOR 2: Yes, I'm ready.

NARRADOR(A) 2: Sí, estoy listo.

NARRATOR 1: Well, tell the world famous detective the story.

NARRADOR(A) 1: Bueno, cuéntale el famoso detective del mundo el cuento.

NARRATOR 2: O.K., here goes. Mary had a little lamb.

NARRADOR(A) 2: Está bien, aquí va. María tenía un pequeño cordero.

DETECTIVE: Let's see if I got that right. This little girl had a pet lamb instead of a pet dog or a pet cat.

DETECTIVE: Déjame ver si lo tengo correcto. Esta pequeña niña tenía un cordero de mascota en vez de un perro o un gato.

NARRATOR 2: Its fleece was white as snow.

NARRADOR(A) 2: Su lana era blanca como la nieve.

DETECTIVE: O.K., so it has a lot of white wool all over its body. It looked just like a walking cloud.

DETECTIVE: Está bien, entonces tiene much lana blanca en todo su cuerpo. Me parece como una nube que camina.

NARRATOR 2: And everywhere that Mary went . . . .

NARRADOR(A) 2: Y a todos los lugares que María iba . . . .

DETECTIVE: So, this Mary person would go to lots of places like the mall, the video store, McDonalds®, and places like that.

DETECTIVE: Entonces, esta María iba a muchos lugares como al centro commercial, la tienda de videos, McDonalds®, y lugares como estos.

NARRATOR 2: The lamb was sure to go.

NARRADOR(A) 2: El cordero iba también.

From *Mother Goose Readers Theatre for Beginning Readers* by Anthony D. Fredericks. Westport, CT: Teacher Ideas Press. Copyright © 2007 by Anthony D. Fredericks.

DETECTIVE: So, the lamb would tag along with this Mary person. It would go where she would go. It liked to get around a lot.

DETECTIVE: Entonces, el cordero iba con esta María. Iba adonde ella iba. Al cordero le gustaba viajar.

NARRATOR 2: It followed her to school one day.

NARRADOR(A) 2: La siguió a la escuela un día.

DETECTIVE: The lamb wanted to be as smart as Mary so it went to her school. Cool!

DETECTIVE: El cordero quería ser tan listo como María y por eso fue a la escuela de ella. ¡Que chévere!

NARRATOR 2: Which was against the rule . . . .

NARRADOR(A) 2: Lo cual era encontra de las reglas . . . .

DETECTIVE: Hey, the school didn't like lambs. I guess they didn't want the lambs making a big mess all over the place.

DETECTIVE: Oye, a la escuela no le gustan los corderos. Supongo que ellos no querían corderos haciendo desorden por todos lados.

NARRATOR 2: It made the children laugh and sing . . . .

NARRADOR(A) 2: Hicieron reir y cantar los niños . . . .

DETECTIVE: Hey, all the kids liked the cute little lamb.

DETECTIVE: Oye, a todos los niños les gustó el lindo pequeño cordero.

NARRATOR 2: Which was against the rule.

NARRADOR(A) 2: Lo cual era encontra de las reglas.

From *Mother Goose Readers Theatre for Beginning Readers* by Anthony D. Fredericks. Westport, CT: Teacher Ideas Press. Copyright © 2007 by Anthony D. Fredericks.

DETECTIVE: Yeah, this Mary person and the lamb animal broke the rule. No animals at school.

DETECTIVE: Sí, esta María y su cordero rompieron la regla. No animales en la escuela.

NARRATOR 1: So, what do you think?

NARRADOR(A) 1: ¿Entonces, qué piensas?

DETECTIVE: I think that Mary should not take any more animals to school. She could take her little brother. She could take her older sister. But she can't take animals.

DETECTIVE: Yo pienso que María no debe llevar más animales a la escuela. Ella llevaría su hermano pequeño. Ella llevaría su hermana mayor. Pero ella no puede llevar animales.

NARRATOR 1: So, now what?

NARRADOR(A) 1: ¿Entonces, qué haces?

DETECTIVE: The case is closed. Mary was bad. The lamb was bad. And, now Mary has to do a lot of homework.

DETECTIVE: El caso está cerrado. María estuvo mal. El cordero estuvo mal. Y, ahora María tiene que hacer mucha tarea.

NARRATOR 1: What kind of homework?

NARRADOR(A) 1: ¿Qué tipo de tarea?

DETECTIVE: She has to clean up after her lamb. Oh, yuck!

DETECTIVE: Ella tiene que limpiar el desorden que hizo el cordero. ¡Qué sucio!

From *Mother Goose Readers Theatre for Beginning Readers* by Anthony D. Fredericks. Westport, CT: Teacher Ideas Press. Copyright © 2007 by Anthony D. Fredericks.

Peter Piper

PRESENTATION SUGGESTIONS

This can be a challenging script for students to read, simply because of all the alliterative words. However, with sufficient practice, it can also be a script filled with fun and laughter. Provide sufficient opportunities for students to practice their lines in advance of a presentation. Note that the names of the players were chosen for alliterative reasons. Feel free to substitute other alliterative names according to the students in your classroom or library program.

PROPS

No props are necessary for this script.

DELIVERY

The first reading of the script should be done at a comfortable rate. The second reading should be at an upbeat and rapid rate. Let students know that they will need to maintain continuity from line to line and from character to character.

ORIGINAL VERSION

Peter Piper picked a peck
Of pickled peppers;
A peck of pickled peppers
Peter Piper picked.

If Peter Piper picked a peck
Of pickled peppers,
Where's the peck of pickled peppers
Peter Piper picked?

COMPREHENSION ACTIVITY(IES)

1. Invite students to create their own illustrations of lots of peppers. These illustrations can be posted on a special bulletin board. In the center of the board can be an illustration of Peter Piper. Take time to discuss the two major points of this Mother Goose rhyme:

    – There were lots and lots of peppers.

    – Peter Piper picked all the peppers.

2. Obtain a large pepper (a bell pepper works best) from your local grocery store. Invite students to observe the pepper as you turn it around and around in your hands. Now, lead them in the following mental imagery activity:

    Close your eyes and imagine yourself standing in a garden. There are lots of vegetables in the garden. Look carefully and you will see rows of corn in the garden. Look over there and you will see some bean plants in the garden. Look and see some watermelons on the ground. Ummmm, watermelons! And if you look very carefully you will see some tall plants along one side of the garden. Those tall plants are pepper plants. There are many peppers on each plant. The peppers are green. See yourself reaching out and picking a pepper from one of the plants. See yourself picking all the peppers from that plant. You are putting all your peppers into a bag. The bag is getting bigger and bigger. The bag is getting heavier and heavier. The bag is filled with lots and lots of peppers. Now, slowly open your eyes and we will listen to a Mother Goose rhyme [or watch a readers theatre play] about a boy named Peter. Like you did in your garden, Peter picks lots and lots of peppers.

Peter Piper

STAGING: The four players should be seated on chairs or tall stools. The narrator should be standing. Note that the audience has a small part at the end.

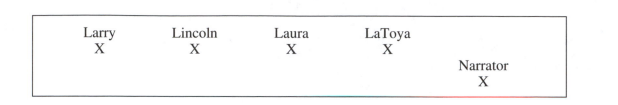

Larry	Lincoln	Laura	LaToya	
X	X	X	X	
				Narrator
				X

NARRATOR: Hi, folks. We have an exciting readers theatre for you today. Our four players [points to the four players] will share a popular Mother Goose rhyme with you. But this is a tricky story. That's because there are many words in the story that begin with the same letter. That makes them hard to say. In fact, almost all the words start with the letter "P." So, let's listen carefully and see how they do.

LARRY: Hey, don't forget about their part [points to audience].

NARRATOR: Thanks, I almost DID forget. We have a part for you [points to audience] in this script. When I point to you, all of you will say "Peter Piper picked." Here is what you will say, again—"Peter Piper picked." O.K.? Are you ready players [points to players]?

ALL PLAYERS: Yes.

NARRATOR: Are you ready audience [points to audience]?

AUDIENCE: Yes.

NARRATOR: Then, let's go. Larry, start us off.

LARRY: Peter Piper

LINCOLN: Picked a peck

LAURA: Of pickled . . .

LaTOYA: peppers;

LARRY: A peck

LINCOLN: of pickled peppers

LAURA: Peter Piper

LaTOYA: picked.

LARRY: If Peter Piper

LINCOLN: picked a peck

LAURA: Of pickled

LaTOYA: peppers

LARRY: Where's

LINCOLN: the peck

LAURA: of pickled

LaTOYA: peppers

[The Narrator points to the audience.]

AUDIENCE: Peter Piper picked?

NARRATOR: O.K., very good. Now, let's do it again. But this time we'll do it really, really fast. Are you ready? O.K., let's go!

[The players will read their parts at a faster clip than in the first round.]

LARRY: Peter Piper

LINCOLN: Picked a peck

LAURA: Of pickled . . .

LaTOYA: peppers;

LARRY: A peck

LINCOLN: of pickled peppers

LAURA: Peter Piper

LaTOYA: picked.

LARRY: If Peter Piper

LINCOLN: picked a peck

LAURA: Of pickled

LaTOYA: peppers

LARRY: Where's

LINCOLN: the peck

LAURA: of pickled

LaTOYA: peppers

[The narrator points to the audience.]

AUDIENCE: Peter Piper picked?

NARRATOR: Congratulations. You did a great job.

 From *Mother Goose Readers Theatre for Beginning Readers* by Anthony D. Fredericks. Westport, CT: Teacher Ideas Press. Copyright © 2007 by Anthony D. Fredericks.

Interesting Facts about Mother Goose

Most Mother Goose rhymes were written in England and have been around for hundreds of years. (All the rhymes in this book are the original English versions.) Some were crafted in response to the actions (or inactions) of English kings and queens. Others were developed as bedtime stories for children. Still others were written as a way to protest the injustices (e.g., high taxes) of the English monarchy.

Suffice it to say, these rhymes have not always been "childlike" in their genesis or in their intent. In my research for this book I learned that many Mother Goose rhymes have multiple interpretations depending on who's being talked about, the social conditions of the time, or the psychological inclinations of the interpreter. I thought that you might enjoy the "history" behind some of the more popular and common rhymes. I will leave to your discretion which of the following tidbits you will want to share with students.

- The term "Mother Goose" has been traced to Loret's 1650 *La Muse Historique,* in which appeared the line, *Comme un conte de la Mere Oye* ("Like a Mother Goose Story").

- "London Bridge" refers to a bridge constructed in the thirteenth century—one that lasted for 600 years. Unfortunately the bridge required constant maintenance and was continuously rebuilt. The current "London Bridge" is now preserved (and maintained) in Arizona.

- In the rhyme "Pop Goes the Weasel," the weasel is a reference to the sound of a spinning machine at the end of its cycle.

- In 1697 Charles Perrault published a collection of eight fairy tales (*Tales of Mother Goose*). The fairy tales included "Cinderella," "Sleeping Beauty," and "Little Red Riding Hood."

- In "This Old Man" a "knick-knack" refers to an insignificant piece of furniture or a minor artifact.

- Little "Jack" Horner was actually Thomas Horner, who lived during the reign of King Henry VIII. The rhyme refers to the way in which he acquired the deed to a "plum" piece of real estate—Mells Manor—in 1536.

- The single most important promoter of the designation of Mother Goose as writer of children's rhymes was John Newbery (after whom the Newbery Award is named).

- One interpretation of "Ring-a-Ring o' Roses" speculated that "we all fall down" is a reference to the high death rate during the time of the Black Death (bubonic plague).

- A much earlier version of "Mary, Mary, Quite Contrary" had the following as its last line: "Sing! Cuckolds all in a row."

- "Ladybird, Ladybird" has several varying interpretations—all religiously based. Suffice it to say, it is one of the most violent Mother Goose rhymes ever.

- May 1 is Mother Goose Day.

- "Yankee Doodle" was a reference to the ineptitude of American soldiers during the Revolutionary War. However, the Americans enjoyed the accompanying music so much that they adopted it as a marching song.

- There are several interpretations of "Jack and Jill." One ribald explanation is that "up the hill to fetch a pail of water" is an old English euphemism for "a roll in the hay."

- In the original version, "Georgy Porgy" was "Rowly Powley"—a reference to an extremely obese child (roly-poly).

- "Curds and whey" is an old term for cottage cheese.

- "Rub-a-dub dub, three men in a tub" was originally "Hey! Rub-a-dub! Ho! Rub-a-dub! Three maids in a tub." The earlier version was inspired by a fairground peep show.

- The origins of "Ding Dong Bell" have been traced back to 1580. The tolling of the bell is a reference to the death of a cat.

- The original "Tweedledum and Tweedledee" predated the Lewis Carroll version in "Through the Looking Glass" by over a century.

- "Pease porridge" is thick pea soup.

- "Baa, Baa, Black Sheep" is an early diatribe against high taxes.

- "Jack Be Nimble" has overtones of fortune-telling. In Buckinghamshire, England, it was considered good luck to be able to leap over a candlestick without extinguishing the flame. It meant one was a healthy individual able to meet the challenges of the year ahead.

- Miss Muffet is said to depict the daughter ("Patience") of noted seventeenth-century entomologist Dr. Thomas Muffet.

- Despite what some people would like to believe, "ride a cock horse to Banbury Cross" is not a reference to Lady Godiva.

- "Little Boy Blue" is a reference to Charles II and all the good times he enjoyed ("under the haystack") while in exile in Europe.

- The official home of The Mother Goose Society is www.librarysupport.net/mothergoosesociety/index.html.

- "Humpty Dumpty" used to be a cannon mounted on the walls of a church in Colchester, England. It was blown up during the English Civil War (1642–1649).

Resources

READERS THEATRE BOOKS

Barchers, S. *Fifty Fabulous Fables: Beginning Readers Theatre*. Westport, CT: Teacher Ideas Press, 1997.

———. *Judge for Yourself*. Westport, CT: Teacher Ideas Press, 2004.

———. *Multicultural Folktales: Readers Theatre for Elementary Students*. Westport, CT: Teacher Ideas Press, 2000.

———. *Readers Theatre for Beginning Readers*. Westport, CT: Teacher Ideas Press, 1993.

———. *Scary Readers Theatre*. Westport, CT: Teachers Ideas Press, 1994.

Barchers, S., and C. R. Pfeffinger. *More Readers Theatre for Beginning Readers*. Westport, CT: Teacher Ideas Press, 2006.

Barnes, J. W. *Sea Songs*. Westport, CT: Teacher Ideas Press, 2004.

Black, A. N. *Born Storytellers*. Westport, CT: Teacher Ideas Press, 2005.

Criscoe, B. L., and P. J. Lanasa. *Fairy Tales for Two Readers*. Westport, CT: Teacher Ideas Press, 1995.

Dixon, N., A. Davies, and C. Politano. *Learning with Readers Theatre: Building Connections*. Winnipeg, Canada: Peguis Publishers, 1996.

Fredericks, A. D. *Frantic Frogs and Other Frankly Fractured Folktales for Readers Theatre*. Westport, CT: Teacher Ideas Press, 1993.

———. *Nonfiction Readers Theatre for Beginning Readers*. Westport, CT: Teacher Ideas Press, 2007.

———. *Readers Theatre for American History*. Westport, CT: Teacher Ideas Press, 2001.

———. *Science Fiction Readers Theatre*. Westport, CT: Teacher Ideas Press, 2002.

———. *Silly Salamanders and Other Slightly Stupid Stories for Readers Theatre*. Westport, CT: Teacher Ideas Press, 2000.

———. *Tadpole Tales and Other Totally Terrific Treats for Readers Theatre*. Westport, CT: Teacher Ideas Press, 1997.

Garner, J. *Wings of Fancy: Using Readers Theatre to Study Fantasy Genre*. Westport, CT: Teacher Ideas Press, 2006.

Georges, C., and C. Cornett. *Reader's Theatre*. Buffalo, NY: D.O.K. Publishers, 1990.

Haven, K. *Great Moments in Science: Experiments and Readers Theatre*. Westport, CT: Teacher Ideas Press, 1996.

Jenkins, D. R. *Just Deal with It*. Westport, CT: Teacher Ideas Press, 2004.

Johnson, T. D., and D. R. Louis. *Bringing It All Together: A Program for Literacy*. Portsmouth, NH: Heinemann, 1990.

Latrobe, K. H., C. Casey, and L. A. Gann. *Social Studies Readers Theatre for Young Adults*. Westport, CT: Teacher Ideas Press, 1991.

Laughlin, M. K., P. T. Black, and K. H. Latrobe. *Social Studies Readers Theatre for Children*. Westport, CT: Teacher Ideas Press, 1991.

Laughlin, M. K., and K. H. Latrobe. *Readers Theatre for Children*.   Westport, CT: Teacher Ideas Press, 1990.

Martin, J. M. *12 Fabulously Funny Fairy Tale Plays*. New York: Instructor Books, 2002.

Peterson, C. *Around the World Through Holidays*. Westport, CT: Teacher Ideas Press, 2005.

Pfeffinger, C. R. *Character Counts*. Westport, CT: Teacher Ideas Press, 2003.

———. *Holiday Readers Theatre*. Westport, CT: Teacher Ideas Press, 1994.

Pugliano-Martin, C. *25 Just-Right Plays for Emergent Readers (Grades K–1)*. New York: Scholastic, 1999.

Shepard, A. *Folktales on Stage: Children's Plays for Readers Theatre*. Olympia, WA: Shepard Publications, 2003.

———. *Readers on Stage: Resources for Readers Theatre*. Olympia, WA: Shepard Publications, 2004.

———. *Stories on Stage: Children's Plays for Readers Theatre*. Olympia, WA: Shepard Publications, 2005.

Sloyer, S. *From the Page to the Stage*. Westport, CT: Teacher Ideas Press, 2003.

Wolf, J. M. *Cinderella Outgrows the Glass Slipper and Other Zany Fractured Fairy Tale Plays*. New York: Scholastic, 2002.

Wolfman, J. *How and Why Stories for Readers Theatre*. Westport, CT: Teacher Ideas Press, 2004.

Worthy, J. *Readers Theatre for Building Fluency: Strategies and Scripts for Making the Most of This Highly Effective, Motivating, and Research-Based Approach to Oral Reading*. New York: Scholastic, 2005.

WEB SITES

http://www.aaronshep.com/rt/RTE.html
How to use readers theatre, sample scripts from a children's author who specializes in readers theatre, and an extensive list of resources.

http://www.cdli.ca/CITE/langrt.htm
This site has lots of information, including What Is Readers Theatre, Readers Theatre Scripts, Writing Scripts, Recommended Print Resources, and Recommended On-line Resources.

http://www.teachingheart.net/readerstheater.htm
Here you'll discover lots of plays and lots of scripts to print and read in your classroom or library.

http://literacyconnections.com/readerstheater
There is an incredible number of resources and scripts at this all-inclusive site.

http://www.proteacher.com/070173.shmtl
> This site is a growing collection of tens of thousands of ideas shared by teachers across the United States and around the world.

http://www.readerstheatredigest.com
> This is an online magazine of ideas, scripts, and teaching strategies.

http://www.readerstheatre.escd.net
> This site has over 150 short poems, stories, and chants for readers theatre.

http://www.storycart.com
> Storycart Press's subscription service provides an inexpensive opportunity to have timely scripts delivered to teachers or librarians each month. Each script is created or adapted by well-known writer Suzanne Barchers, author of several readers theatre books (see above).

PROFESSIONAL ORGANIZATION

Institute for Readers Theatre
P.O. Box 421262
San Diego, CA 92142
(858) 277-4274
http://www.readerstheatreinstitute.com

Teacher Resources

by

Anthony D. Fredericks

The following books are available from Teacher Ideas Press (88 Post Road West, Westport, CT 06881); 1-800-225-5800; http://www.teacherideaspress.com.

Frantic Frogs and Other Frankly Fractured Folktales for Readers Theatre. ISBN 1-56308-174-1. (123pp.; $19.50).
> Have you heard "Don't Kiss Sleeping Beauty, She's Got Really Bad Breath" or "The Brussels Sprouts Man (The Gingerbread Man's Unbelievably Strange Cousin)"? This resource (grades 4–8) offers 30 reproducible satirical scripts for rip-roaring dramatics in any classroom or library.

The Integrated Curriculum: Books for Reluctant Readers, Grades 2–5. **2nd ed.** ISBN 0-87287-994-1. (220pp.; $22.50).
> This book presents guidelines for motivating and using literature with reluctant readers. The book contains more than 40 book units on titles carefully selected to motivate the most reluctant readers.

Investigating Natural Disasters Through Children's Literature: An Integrated Approach. ISBN 1-56308-861-4. (193pp.; $28.00).
> Tap into students' inherent awe of storms, volcanic eruptions, hurricanes, earthquakes, tornadoes, floods, avalanches, landslides, and tsunamis to open their minds to the wonders and power of the natural world. .

Involving Parents Through Children's Literature: P–K. ISBN 1-56308-022-2. (86pp.; $15.00).

Involving Parents Through Children's Literature: Grades 1–2. ISBN 1-56308-012-5. (95pp.; $14.50).

Involving Parents Through Children's Literature: Grades 3–4. ISBN 1-56308-013-3. (96pp.; $15.50).

Involving Parents Through Children's Literature: Grades 5–6. ISBN 1-56308-014-1. (107pp.; $16.00).
> This series of four books offers engaging activities for adults and children that stimulate comprehension and promote reading enjoyment. Reproducible activity sheets based upon high-quality children's books are designed in a convenient format so that children can take them home.

The Librarian's Complete Guide to Involving Parents Through Children's Literature: Grades K–6. ISBN 1-56308-538-0. (137pp.; $24.50).
> Activities for 101 children's books are presented in a reproducible format, so librarians can distribute them to students to take home and share with parents.

MORE Social Studies Through Children's Literature: An Integrated Approach. ISBN 1-56308-761-8. (225pp.; $27.50).

    Energize your social studies curriculum with dynamic, "hands-on, minds-on" projects based on such great children's books as *Amazing Grace*, *Fly Away Home*, and *Lon Po Po*. This books is filled with an array of activities and projects sure to "energize" any social studies curriculum.

Much More Social Studies Through Children's Literature: A Collaborative Approach. ISBN 1-59158-445-0. (278pp.; $35.00).

Nonfiction Readers Theatre for Beginning Readers. ISBN 1-59158-499-X. (220pp.; $25.00).

    This collection of science and social studies nonfiction scripts for beginning readers is sure to "jazz up" any language arts program in grades 1–3. Teachers and librarians will discover a wealth of creative opportunities to enhance fluency, comprehension, and appreciate of nonfiction literature.

Readers Theatre for American History. ISBN 1-56308-860-6. (173pp.; $30.00).

    This book offers a participatory approach to American history in which students become active participants in several historical events. These 24 scripts give students a "you are there" perspective on critical milestones and colorful moments that have shaped the American experience.

Science Adventures with Children's Literature: A Thematic Approach. ISBN 1-56308-417-1. (190pp.; $24.50).

    Focusing on the National Science Education Standards, this activity-centered resource uses a wide variety of children's literature to integrate science across the elementary curriculum. With a thematic approach, it features the best in science trade books along with stimulating hands-on, minds on activities in all the sciences.

Science Discoveries on the Net: An Integrated Approach. ISBN 1-56308-823-1. (315pp.; $27.50).

    This book is designed to help teachers integrate the Internet into their science programs and enhance the scientific discoveries of students. The 88 units emphasize key concepts—based on national and state standards—throughout the science curriculum.

Silly Salamanders and Other Slightly Stupid Stuff for Readers Theatre. ISBN 1-56308-825-8. (161pp.; $23.50).

    The third entry in the "wild and wacky" readers theatre trilogy is just as crazy and just as weird as the first two. This unbelievable resource offers students in grades 3–6 dozens of silly send-ups of well-known fairy tales, legends and original stories.

Social Studies Discoveries on the Net: An Integrated Approach. ISBN 1-56308-824-X. (276pp.; $26.00).

    This book is designed to help teachers integrate the Internet into their social studies programs and enhance the classroom discoveries of students. The 75 units emphasize key concepts – based on national and state standards – throughout the social studies curriculum.

Social Studies Through Children's Literature: An Integrated Approach. ISBN 1-87287-970-4. (192pp.; $24.00).

    Each of the 32 instructional units contained in this resource utilizes an activity-centered approach to elementary social studies, featuring children's picture books such as *Ox-Cart Man*, *In Coal Country*, and *Jambo Means Hello*.

Tadpole Tales and Other Totally Terrific Titles for Readers Theatre. ISBN 1-56308-547-X. (115pp.; $18.50)

A follow-up volume to the best selling *Frantic Frogs and Other Frankly Fractured Folktales for Readers Theatre*, this book provides primary level readers (grades 1–4) with a humorous assortment of wacky tales based on well-known Mother Goose rhymes. More than 30 scripts and dozens of extensions will keep students rolling in the aisles.

Index